Irving Place Editions

Also by Paul Cody

Shooting the Heart [2004]

So Far Gone [1998]

Eyes Like Mine [1996]

The Stolen Child [1995]

The Last Next Time

a memoir

Paul Cody

Paul Cody
August 2013

Irving Place Editions

Dartmouth MA

Cover photography by Paul Cody
Cover design by John Lauricella
Interior design by John Lauricella

ISBN:
ISBN-10:
Printed and bound on demand in the United States of America.

The Last Next Time is the second publication of Irving Place Editions.
Suspend Your Disbelief—*Read On!*
www.irvingplaceeditions.com

First Edition

This is for

Doug Green

Dr. Adam Law

Dr. Joseph Troncale

Every life is many days, day after day. We walk through ourselves, meeting robbers, ghosts, giants, old men, young men, wives, widows, brothers-in-love. But always meeting ourselves.

~ *Ulysses*

I had never known, never even imagined for a heartbeat, that there might be a place for people like us.

~ Denis Johnson
Jesus' Son

The Last Next Time

For Phoebus —

with love + squalor —

Paul

1

There were things in the fog and rain, in the distance, or
there seemed to be. There were cows and horses. There
were fences and roads. Silos, fields, trees, houses, and signs. Signs
for cars, hamburgers, ice cream, scrap metal. For GIRLS GIRLS
GIRLS, Keystone beer, All-Night Every Night, 24-7. WHAT YOU
WANT WHEN YOU WANT IT.

We were in the car, in steady rain, in the hills of Pennsylvania,
my wife driving, holding a tiny plastic bag with five two m.g. tablets of clonazepam. Tiny white tablets, smaller and flatter than
aspirin.

The wipers whacked at the windshield, and the side windows
were fogged in and streaked with rain. Cars and trucks were gliding waves of color—green, blue, silver, black, red. Some went fast,
some slow.

An eighteen-wheeler went by with gigantic lettuce, tomatoes,
carrots, celery and peppers painted on the side. The produce was
glistening with drops of water, but I couldn't tell if the water was
on our car window, the side of the truck, or in the picture.

Squinting, I stared at the truck for a long time. Then it sped up and was out of sight.

I tapped on the window with my forefinger, one, two, three, four. All I could tell for sure was that I was here, in this car, and I was pretty certain we were headed to rehab, to Caron Treatment Center, in a town called Wernersville, just outside Reading, Pennsylvania.

My wife's face was tired and drawn. While I had been sleeping twelve hours a day, Liz had been sleeping five or six. While I spent much of my time in my third-floor office at home, taking pills, listening to music, reading here and there, cruising the internet, checking email, looking for the mailman to see if he had delivered still another flat, ten-by-twelve envelope from somewhere in the world with still more pills, she was going to work, buying groceries, doing laundry, working on a book, looking after two teenage boys, driving them to friends' houses, to get jeans or sneakers, to running practice or choral concerts.

Liz went to the gym or ran nearly every morning. She had never been high in her life. She had graduated Phi Beta Kappa from college, and won a fellowship to grad school at Cornell. She had published two books of poetry and two novels for young adults.

When I asked the time, Liz said, "Ten till eleven."

I could have a clonazepam at eleven.

We left home in Ithaca, New York, at nine.

There was an old decaying house, with empty windows like missing teeth, and a thin tree growing through the roof. I kept looking, even once it had passed, and wasn't sure if I had seen or imagined the tree, or if it had been something from a memory or dream. Like a thing you see in a cloud.

The past week had been like that. Hours and days—floating in clouds. But there were moments of utter clarity.

The search for a rehab online, where web sites sometimes showed gorgeous couples, slim, well dressed, walking a beach at sunset, riding horses, playing golf. Handsome young men climbed mountains, sailed, smiled at lovely young women. Was this rehab or Club Med?

But the more we looked the more often two names came up— Hazelden and Caron. Both were among the oldest treatment centers in the country, neither offered beaches, golf, or horses as part of the basic regimen. Both, in fact, were known to be quite rigorous and fairly spartan, though each had a high staff to patient ratio and both were expensive.

Hazelden and Caron had satellites around the country, but their main campuses were in St. Paul, Minnesota, and Wernersville, Pennsylvania. Hazelden would require airplane tickets, Caron would not.

According to MapQuest, we were 222 miles from Wernersville.

When I spoke to an admissions woman at Caron, she told me it cost $27,000 for a month. I thought she meant $2700.

$27,000, she said. $27,000.

I had stared out the windows in front of my desk on the third floor. Trees were beginning to leaf out, and kids, singly and in groups of two and three and more, were walking home from school on the street below, carrying backpacks and jackets and sweatshirts. Parents were walking kids, walking dogs. One balding father carried a toddler in a backpack, held the hand of a first- or second-grade girl, and walked a brown spaniel.

It seemed as though I was looking through smeared binoculars.

This was May, and my year of teaching literature and creative writing at Hobart and William Smith Colleges had ended a week earlier. I taught long classes on Wednesdays and Fridays and took low doses of benzos on days of classes. And in a final big push before rehab, I took ten benzos or less for three straight days in order to correct final papers and portfolios, then asked a friend to drive me to my college office so I could leave the corrected work in boxes outside my office door.

I entered grades online, very carefully, from my home office.

Hobart William Smith was in Geneva, New York, a spectacular fifty-mile drive between two enormous Finger Lakes, through farm country and past wineries, with a single traffic light the whole way, once outside the cities of Ithaca and Geneva. The views of lakes and farms, valleys and hills, the changing seasons, Amish homesteads, made the commute a thrill.

In the last weeks of the spring semester, even with the reduction in benzo intake, and with two or three large coffees in my system, my reflexes were slowing, I was sometimes seeing double, and when I walked between the car and my office or between classes, I occasionally experienced dizziness and vertigo. I knew I shouldn't be driving. It was crazy to drive. I had nightmares about killing somebody.

The rain had slowed to a drizzle, but the traffic had increased. We were on Interstate 81, which we had picked up in New York, thirty miles from Ithaca, and now there were signs for Clarks Summit, Dickson City and Scranton. There were signs for Interstates 476, 380 and 84.

"Can I've a clonnie?" I asked.

Liz checked the clock on the dashboard then nodded.

She began to fumble in the small plastic bag in her lap.

"Just gimme the bag," I said.

"I don't think so."

I felt an instant of anger.

"Why?"

She had a tight smile on her face.

The car slowed.

Snowed as I was, I thought, Right. Get used to it. Of course.

When she handed me the small white pill, I felt happy as Christmas.

I stared at the white tablet in the palm of my hand. I put it between my thumb and forefinger. Then slowly, I brought it to my mouth, put it on my tongue, said to myself, Thank you, Liz. Thank you, God.

Then I leaned back, my head against the headrest, and thought I felt the tablet melt slowly, and the calm from the pill entering my blood and tissue and brain.

A yellow car outside the window seemed to slow and float. Another cloud.

The rain had picked up again, was making a steady patter on the roof of the car and on the windows. We seemed to be driving through shallow puddles. There were more watery signs for Scranton, and that meant we were halfway to Caron, and there were still four clonazepam left.

Four was almost less than nothing. Four was enough to take with morning coffee in my former life, enough to keep off the morning shakes, but this was not my former life.

Two nights before my wife and I had gone to my attic office and had carefully gone through every hiding place, looking for drugs and anything associated with drugs. We had found my Miniteller, about the size of a rectangular box of dental floss, with a wire coming out of it. The wire plugged into the USB port on my computer, and when I bought pills online, I could swipe my bank debit card in the Miniteller, punch in my PIN number, and have my payment go directly to the vendor, and I'd get a discount on pills.

Liz and I cut the cord of the Miniteller and threw it out. We found every hiding place for pills, behind my many shelves of books, behind dictionaries and papers and a printer, pills in blister-strips of ten. I kept them in separate baggies. 160 blue Valium. 150 clonazepam. 80 tiny yellow lorazepam. 100 temazepam. We cut the pills out of the strips and pressed them through the aluminum, and flushed all but thirty clonazepan down the toilet.

I confined everything to my third-floor office.

Although I never sold a pill in my life, I kept so many pills on hand because I was afraid to go through withdrawal, a nightmare that could end in seizures and death.

When my supplies got down to two hundred pills or less I was filled with dread and a terrible foreboding. I'd try hard to limit my intake to ten pills or less a day, but sometimes I'd be so anxious about the low supply, that my intake would increase. I'd order more pills online, but because I never quite knew where they were coming from—India? Argentina? Mexico?—and because I didn't know if they would be seized by U.S. Customs, I'd make a few orders and hope one would arrive in ten or twelve days.

If it didn't, withdrawal set in. I'd take to bed, and begin twitching, trembling, hoping not to have a seizure. I wouldn't sleep for a long time. I'd think that I was hallucinating, or that time and place were doing funny things. Swimming underwater, backing up and repeating themselves, going sideways, talking backwards, speaking different languages, loud-soft, loud-soft.

I'd fall asleep very lightly, and if a car backfired somewhere outside, it sounded like a bomb, and if a dog barked it was a gunshot, and the voices of children were tormented.

In the past I had withdrawn from alcohol and narcotics, and that had been straightforward. It was mostly a physical thing, and was over in five or ten days. Benzos were a whole other level of long and scary.

Because the body stores benzodiazepines in muscle and tissue and fat, and because diazepam and clonazepam are two of the longest acting varieties, withdrawal can last months, even a year or more. The withdrawal wears people down—the insomnia, the intense anxiety, the feeling of depersonalization, and the sense, say, in the seventh month, that this is just not going to end.

And this from a family of drugs that is widely believed to be so friendly and benign that it can likely be found in the home of one out of five Americans.

Benzos are most often used medically for the treatment of anxiety and insomnia.

"How you think the boys are?" I asked. We were coming up a long slow hill, and it was now drizzling. Liz had turned the windshield wipers to intermittent. They slapped across the glass every twenty seconds or so.

"I don't know," Liz said. "Okay this morning, before school." She brushed hair from her cheek. "They didn't say much. But they usually don't at that hour."

I had slept in, but each had come to our bedroom, had come around to the side of the bed, bent down to kiss me on the side of the face and say, "I love you, Dad."

I remembered a time, somewhere in the last year, when I'd been laid out in bed for days, from depression or withdrawal or exhaustion, and one of the boys came into the dark bedroom and lay down on the bed next to me. "You okay? You're not sick, are you? You're not dying or something?" Liam asked, or Austin asked. I couldn't remember who.

At the top of the hill we passed a long silver milk truck that had passed us at the bottom of the hill, and ahead there was a valley below a break in the clouds. A village. Ponds, farms, silos, a school with a playground, a baseball field. Churches, a cemetery with small gray headstones, trees, clusters of flowers and American flags.

The village seemed really far away.

"How much damage I do?"

"Hard to tell. You kept to your office."

My office was big, was lined on two long sides with bookshelves that were eleven inches deep, so books could be stacked two-deep. There was a six-foot long trestle table for a desk that stood in front of two windows that looked out onto the street in front of the house. Skylights, a stereo system with three speakers, boxes of CDs, a phone, an IMac computer with a large monitor on the desk. There were Buddhist prayer flags on the wall, prints of the work of John Singer Sargent, Kandinsky, Miró, and Paul Klee. There were seven dictionaries, three complete Shakespeares, two copies of Proust's *The Past Recaptured,* and three copies of *Ulysses.*

There was a copy *of True Crime: 350 Years of Brilliant Writing About Dark Deeds,* edited by Harold Schechter.

My office was a fine and private place. There was a single steep staircase that led up to it from the second-floor hallway. It had a doorway on the second floor. And once on the third floor, other people rarely came upstairs.

In the car, I said, "But you don't see any really awful, permanent things going on?"

Liz looked quickly over, and then back at the road.

The clock on the dashboard read 12:49. Just over ten minutes to another clonazepam.

I thought I'd had eight before we left Ithaca. I'd had another one at 10:00, one at 11:00, one at noon. I was pretty sure there were three left.

"I don't think so," Liz said. "They do well in school, they have plenty of friends, they adore you." She shrugged. "Just worry about you getting off this stuff."

Beautiful, deep green countryside went past. Cows and horses standing patiently in rain. Black roads winding up the side of fields. Knotted trees.

"I don't know," I said. "I'm sorry. I'll be glad to get clean. I just don't look forward to it."

Then we were silent a while, and rural Pennsylvania went past the windows.

I kept trying to imagine rehab. I'd never been to one, and it was hard for me to imagine.

Maybe some people would wear sports jackets and ascots. They would be doctors, lawyers, business leaders, corporate kingpins. Or maybe those people would go to the places with horses and skiing. What did I know? They wouldn't go to the kind of place I'd go to.

"How many miles we on?" I asked.

"You mean, how many have we gone?"

My eyes were closed, and now all I could feel was the whine of the engine, and bumps in the road that I sensed when the car worked its way up a slight or steeper hill, or when Liz touched the brakes.

"Yeah."

My eyes opened a sliver, and I saw Liz glance at the odometer. She looked very pretty. I thought of how we'd been married more than twenty years, and wondered if she wanted to be with me.

"One seventy-seven."

"How many to go?

"Forty-three."

When I closed my eyes I thought of times when I was so snowed by pills, by diazepam, say, and I'd be crawling on my hands and knees on the floor of my office, unable to stand upright, much less walk. And I'd be unable to utter a single coherent word. Not one. Not yes, no, please, not even, help.

A dozen or more years earlier, when my oldest son, Liam, was around a year old, and the absolute thrill of witnessing his first word and first step. He said, Juice, then, weeks later, he put a blanket over a teddy bear and said, Bear sleep.

I'd been so stupefied by benzos, that I had neither of the skills he had mastered at age one.

The rain was gone, but the fog thickened as though the clouds themselves had lowered.

I asked Liz for a clonazepam, and without looking at the clock, she handed the plastic bag to me. There were two tablets left.

I took one and handed it back, feeling virtuous, and swallowed the one with water. "Can I have the last one when we get there? Like in the parking lot?"

"Sure," she said, and I swelled with warmth for her.

We had come off the smaller highway, and were passing houses, buildings, shopping strips, cemeteries, used car lots with pennants hanging wetly from string. I asked Liz how far, and she said, "Two oh three down, less than twenty to go."

We entered a small town, brick buildings, storefronts, a traffic light, through and out the other side.

Staring at a blue house on a hill, I almost flinched.

I was in my office at home and had been drinking beer, and taking more and more and more benzos, and I'd been doing it for several days. It was a weekday, and Liz and the boys were at work and school.

Sitting alone in the bright room, I was revolted by myself. I was so overwhelmed by the addiction, so owned and enslaved by it, that I was never going to stop.

I would end this now. Get the fucking thing finished.

I stood up, walked downstairs and got a white plastic trash bag.

Back upstairs, I lay down on my side on the futon in the corner. I pulled my knees toward my chest. Pulled the bag over my head, secured it at my neck.

There in the car, I looked over, and Liz was driving.

We came up a long hill to an expanse of gorgeous grounds, with white slatted fences like a horse farm, old sandstone buildings, one with a belvedere on top. Some glassy modern buildings as well.

Caron.

We followed signs. Parked in front of a sign that said Admissions, and a building that looked like a large ranch house, only this one went on and on.

Liz parked, I took the last white pill, and Liz took the plastic bag, crushed it, and threw it on the car floor.

"Can we sit a minute?"

"Not too long," she said.

I watched the door to admissions. Nobody went in, nobody came out.

Liz got out, took my bag from the back seat, came around to my side. She stood there.

I opened the door, got unsteadily to my feet, started to say something, stopped.

What could I say? There was nothing to say. Not a word.

2

Inside, a woman sat behind a desk. Beyond her was a waiting room like in an upscale doctor's office. There was lounge art, and the lighting was soft like a funeral home.

The woman gave each of us clipboards with pens, and papers to fill out. I had only one to complete, Liz had quite a few.

I was watching Liz when a woman with short dark hair came in, sat down, crossed her legs and stared at the carpet. She may have been forty years old, there were streaks in her hair that were almost red, and she looked coiled and muscular like a dancer. Her face might have been pretty, but it was tight and white and worried. A muscle worked in her jaw, and there were dark patches under her eyes, and though her slacks were pressed, her maroon scarf looked like silk, her black boots carefully and elegantly stitched, she looked like she had had a bad run.

"Ms. Blanco," the woman behind the desk said.

The woman with dark hair looked up.

"You're all set," the desk woman said.

The dark-haired woman said thank you and walked out.

So. Here in Admissions. Here in the waiting room. So.

I guessed this was where we paid the twenty-seven thousand dollars. We planned to do this with two different credit cards and a check. Kind of spread it around a little. Get some frequent flyer miles, or L.L. Beans bonus points.

There were corridors behind doors, and doors behind doors, but I could neither see nor hear any signs of life.

"What do you think patients look like?" I asked Liz.

Liz looked up. "Excuse me?"

"The patients," I said. "What do you think they look like?"

"Like you," she said. "Like me. Like anybody."

"Oh."

"Whad'ja think they'd look like?" She smiled. She didn't look angry.

"Furtive. Twitchy. Kinda down."

Liz bobbed her head, nodding and moving it from side to side at the same time. Yes, no, sort of.

"Maybe they wear hair shirts," Liz said, "with black and white stripes, and a big A on the chest." She was smiling.

"What's the A for?"

"Addict. Alcoholic."

Somehow over the years, maybe after we had kids, Liz and I had begun to pay less attention to each other. We each worked, me as a teacher, Liz as a speechwriter at Cornell. We drove kids to school, to friends' houses, we read to them, talked to and listened to the kids, took turns watching them. The rare times we were alone, we talked about the kids.

We hadn't been out to a movie in years, rarely went out to dinner, and while she was asleep at ten each night, I stayed up until one or two, savoring the lovely silence.

In the waiting room, we sat for a few minutes, then a door to a long hallway opened.

A woman with black glasses introduced herself as Robin from Admissions.

"If I can speak to you first, Paul, then you, Liz, that would be great."

I handed my clipboard to the woman behind the desk, and followed Robin through several glass doors that snapped heavily behind us.

Robin wore a dark blue blazer over a white blouse, black slacks, and shoes with a serious heel. A heel so serious I didn't quite understand how she could walk. Her ankle kind of bowed out with each step.

We passed offices with closed doors, and Robin fumbled through keys, unlocked and held open the door for me. Medium-sized office, a poster on the wall of four rowers in a scull, mist on a river, then two windows, desk, chairs, computer, phone.

"Paul, I just need to ask you a few questions, okay? Very basic."

"Sure."

"Who are you?"

"Paul Cody."

"Where are we?"

"Caron Treatment Center, in Wernersville, Pennsylvania."

"Good. And what day is this?"

"It's Thursday afternoon, May 14, 2009."

"Very good. Do you know what we just did?"

"Yeah, you just tested to see if I was oriented in all three spheres, as to person, place and time."

"Correct."

"So I'm not crazy?"

She shook her head, then asked if I'd send Liz in.

Liz had finished the paperwork and was looking at the floor, examining the carpet or the toes of her shoes. She didn't look as tired as she'd looked driving.

She stood up and went through the door. I walked to a window and watched the drizzle fall on trees and parked cars. It was not a heavy but a steady rain, and it made everything soaked and shiny, sad and somber.

After a while, Liz touched my shoulder lightly, and said it was time to go to the Medical Unit, where we would say goodbye. She said it was next door, so we went through more doorways, down halls, and found a hallway corner with a glassed-in nurses' station. It had sliding windows, and three nurses working behind computers.

I stood in front of one of the nurses, who was probably my age, mid-fifties, and had long blond hair. She wore a nametag that said Peggy, and glasses hung down her front on a brown cord. There was a pen behind her ear.

"Be right with you, Paul," she said, and I was astonished she knew my name.

As I stood in front of the window I realized that I was swaying as I stood. I could tell from lining myself up with the vertical silver dividers between each pane of glass. I was moving slowly from side to side.

"Liz, you want to say goodbye to Paul now, and then we can get started with his intake and taper?"

Liz turned to hug me, and I somehow hadn't realized she'd been carrying my big black bag, which she'd set near her feet. I nearly fell over it, then took the bag. "Sorry," she said, and I said, "No, I'm sorry, really."

Then there were tears in her eyes, and she blinked them back.

"You'll be fine," she said, and I didn't know if that was a question or reassurance. "Get well."

"Yeah."

Someone wearing sweats went by in the hall.

I said, "Drive safe."

We let go, patted each other's upper arms, looked each other in the eyes.

She went down the hall, her footsteps short and fast, and through the outside door, lean as she'd been the day we were married.

Peggy said, "All set."

She looked unfazed. She was barely over five feet tall, and I towered over her.

She led me to a room with a scale, examination table, an upright blood pressure machine. "Could you take your shoes off so I can weigh you, please?"

I took off my reddish Danskos, got on the scale, started to move the weights on the bar. Two-hundred, two-oh-seven.

A poster on the wall was about hydration.

Peggy asked me to measure myself on the scale, and I pushed the stick up on the back of it. I was somewhere between six one and a half and six two.

Then I sat in a chair, she wrapped a blood pressure cuff around my arm, pumped it. One eighteen over sixty eight. She held my wrist, looked at her watch. Pulse: 70.

She took two tubes of blood from my arm, then asked me questions about diet, sex, exercise, diseases, family history, hospitalization, children, spouse, drug use, drinking, medication.

"Okay, kiddo," she said, "if you could wait in the lounge, Dr. Troncale will see you shortly."

"The lounge?" I said.

"Right opposite the nurses' station." She looked at me a long moment. "Good luck," she said.

There were three people in the lounge: a woman sleeping deeply on a couch under a red blanket, a guy sitting on another couch, about sixty, with a goofy smile, who tried to stand up to shake my hand but sank back onto the couch, and a young woman, possibly twenty, with a bandaged wrist and lank brown hair who sat in a chair in front of windows. She stared at a television that played *Young Frankenstein* without the sound.

I sat in a chair near the door.

"Dude," the guy said. "You just in?" He had a crazy smile. He sounded like a surfer, say, from Malibu or Santa Cruz.

I nodded. "You?"

"Couple a days," he said. "I think." Then he laughed and coughed.

He had one of those cigarettes and whiskey voices, rough and smooth and old, all at once. A voice with years and miles on it, one you heard in bars late at night.

"What's your drug of choice?" he asked. "If you don't mind my asking."

"Not at all," I said. "A little of lots of things. Mostly benzos."

He nodded. He tried to stand again, got halfway up, then sat down fast. "Getting old," he said.

"Getting detoxed," the woman near the windows said.

We looked at her.

"Heroin," she said.

"What?" I asked.

"I did heroin."

"You're too young to do heroin."

"Listen, chickadee." She had cloudy brown eyes. "Everyone at boarding school did coke, crank or smack."

"She's right," a girl's voice said.

I turned, and the sleeping girl was looking at us from under a mess of blanket, sweater and hair. "Sara's right. Everyone does shit."

I stared.

"Don't worry, dude," Sara said. "You're old. You're not supposed to know."

"My name's Paul," I said. I wanted to say something I was sure of.

The sleeping girl sat up, pushed hair out of her face. She looked about sixteen. She was thin and oddly elegant in a tired kind of way.

The door opened, and a dark-haired girl stood in the doorway smiling.

"There's my girl," Sara said, and the new girl said, "Hey," and everybody but me said, Hey.

"You a new guy?" she asked me, and I said, "Yeah." She shook my hand. I could feel bones. "Liana," she said.

"Pain pills, right?" she said.

"Benzos."

"Heroin."

"Boarding school?"

"How'd you know?"

"The good manners."

She laughed. She had perfect teeth.

She seemed to be about fifteen or sixteen, and there was something very old and very young about her. She was tall, her hair cut chin-length, and she had a smile that reached her eyes.

"By the way, Phil," the man on the couch said.

"His name's Paul," the sleeping girl said.

"You were sleeping," Sara said.

"I was sleeping, but I heard."

"Pete, Phil, Paul," the man on the couch said.

"Dammit," the sleeping girl said, "shut up."

"Park," he said.

"What the hell kind of name is that?" Liana said. "That's where you take a walk."

"Or sell drugs." Sara laughed.

The sleeping girl said, "Do drugs."

"Paul," he said.

I said, "Yes."

"My name's Gavin. It means white hawk in Welsh."

Gavin looked a long way from a white hawk in any language. Gavin couldn't rise to his feet.

"Great," I said. "Drug of choice?" In here, it seemed like asking what someone did for a living. Instead of lawyer or carpenter or student, it was smack or speed, booze or benzos.

"Coke and booze," Gavin said.

"I like coke," Sara said.

I wondered what Liana was thinking.

She was sitting on the far side of me, near the television. She looked even younger in the light from the windows.

There was a knock on the door and a nurse came in. She had light brown hair, looked to be in her early thirties, and had pale skin and freckles. "Julie, Sara, time to go over to Women's."

"Oh man," Julie said.

"C'mon," the nurse said. She was tall, and blinked as though something was painful.

Sara and Julie left with her.

"See ya," Liana said after the door clicked shut.

Gavin was sleeping.

There was silence for what seemed a long time. Silence but for rain. Silence with clicks, hums, snaps and beeps. Distant voices behind doors, breath, maybe heartbeats.

After a while Liana asked me if I had any cigarettes. I said I did and gave her two or three. Her fingers were very long, pale and almost unlined. She said thanks, then told me I wasn't supposed to give her cigarettes. I asked why, and she said cause she was female, underage, and that we could both get kicked out.

Her eyes were sad, not in a broken way, but in a way of knowing things she shouldn't have known.

"How old are you?"

"Fifteen."

"I'm sorry."

"Why?

"So young."

She touched my arm. "I'm leaving in a week. Going to a place in Baltimore. A fancy mental hospital, Sheppard-Pratt."

Her eyes were like clear sky.

Then we were quiet, and we listened to Gavin snore, and after a while Liana asked me what I thought Gavin was dreaming about.

"Really dry martinis, and lines of coke on a mirror."

A nurse opened the door. "Paul. Dr. Troncale."

I waved to Liana, who gave me a small, secret wave, barely moving her fingers.

We went down one hallway, took a right, passed a number of doorways. She stopped at a door halfway down, knocked, said, "I have Paul to see you."

An answering voice said, "Come in."

I thanked the nurse. She closed the door, and I was shaking hands with a white-haired, friendly-looking man.

"Sit down, Paul. How are you?"

"I'm okay."

He looked at me, nodding for a few moments.

The room wasn't big.

Inside was a file cabinet, bookcases with framed photos of smiling people at what looked like weddings and graduations, young women and men. There were books, diplomas, three-ring binders. There were pictures on the walls, charts, drawings by kids.

"So," Dr. Troncale said.

"Hmmm," I said.

"Okay. Now let me get this straight. I have your information, but I want to get it from you. You've had long periods of sobriety?"

"Twenty-five years."

"Wow."

"Twenty-three to forty-eight."

"Good for you. What happened?"

"Had a drink."

There was a bird in the rain, outside the window.

"Then?"

He held on to the word then, stretched it out, turned it into two syllables like a Southerner.

"Well, I guess, I think, I stayed away from booze for the most part, but a shrink gave me lorazepam. I was real depressed and anxious. It helped."

"How much?"

"One hundred sixty pills, .25 milligrams each. They helped. But that was the start."

He shook his head, looked at the computer screen.

"I should have known better," I added.

"We make mistakes." He looked at me and he was smiling. "You got this disease and you make that mistake and it can kill you."

He looked at the keyboard a minute. "How you feeling now? In terms of withdrawal?"

"I'm okay."

"Paul, I need you to do something for me." He looked over at me, his eyes serious. "You don't like to ask for help, do you?"

"What?"

"You don't like to ask for help, do you?"

"What do you mean?"

"Simple question. You don't like to ask for help, do you?"

"I don't."

"Thank you. Didn't know if I was gonna get that."

He took out his wallet, opened it, took out a dollar bill.

"I want to give you something," he said.

"I'm getting suspicious," I said.

He laughed.

The bird was gone from outside the window.

He offered me the dollar bill. "This is for you," he said.

"I don't want it," I said.

"I want you to take it," he said.

"I don't want it. I don't need it."

"Please take it."

"I don't want it."

"Here's a dollar for you. Please take it."

"I'll take it if you sign it."

He did, and I did.

"Okay, good. Now we got that out of the way."

He tapped at the keyboard of his computer. His reading glasses were at the end of his nose. He said, "How much clonazepam and diazepam were you taking a day? On average?"

"I'd spike up to forty or fifty, but on average it was more like twenty-five, thirty a day, of 2 milligram or 10 milligram."

He nodded, without looking up.

Dr. Troncale wrote on a square of paper. "Here's what we have for you," he said. "Four 2 m.g. of Ativan four times a day for three days. Then drop to three 2 m.g. three times a day for three days, then three 1 m.g. three times for three days, then 1 m.g. before bed for three days."

I nodded.

There were pictures on the walls. Diplomas. A window. A jacket hung on the back of a closet door. There was a desk, a computer, a phone. A few chairs.

"Can I ask a question?"

"Of course."

"Is this real? Is this happening?"

He looked at me. "Let me ask you something?" He paused. Large brown eyes. "When you had thirty pills in you, in your muscle, tissue, your brain, was that real? Was that happening?"

3

The room in the Medical Unit wasn't like an ordinary hospital room. There were no curtains around the beds, no tall trays on wheels, none of the silver panels on the wall above the bed where things could be plugged in. There were two beds, one on the window side of the room where a guy with dark stringy hair snored lightly. I was in the bed near the hall door, and opposite the foot of the bed there was a bathroom with yellow tiles.

The room was dark except for a nightlight under the windows.

They gave me four 2 m.g. Ativan, and that made me tired for some reason, even though eight milligrams was not much, and Ativan or lorazepam was a short-acting benzo, and compared to clonazepam or diazepam it was not especially strong. But I slept like I meant to sleep forever.

A short, middle-aged nurse did wake me, sometime in the dark, at ten at night or four in the morning.

She said her said her name was Suzanne, and she said I should get up to go to the bathroom because I hadn't gone in a while. My stomach was suddenly roiling as though I'd eaten bad clams, and as I lurched toward the bathroom door it seemed as though my stomach was racing up through my chest, my throat, my mouth, and then an amorphous ball, maybe the size of a softball, shot out of my mouth, flew across the room, and exploded and turned liquid against the tiles above the toilet.

It was green and black and silvery, and was so fast and surprising that I said, "What?"

"Projectile vomiting," Suzanne said.

I wiped streaks of vomit off the toilet, tried to but couldn't throw up more. Then I washed my hands and face, and sat on the edge of the bed.

Suzanne came back with a small can of ginger ale, crackers, and a blood pressure cuff. She took my blood pressure and pulse, said ginger ale and crackers might help settle my stomach.

"You all right?" she asked.

I nodded. "Just very tired."

I got under the covers. She patted my shoulder, said get some sleep, and I listened to her going out.

The tiredness felt sweet and deep. The bed was firm, the snoring a ticking clock. I closed my eyes, and for a minute or more I saw a green-black ball move in the air toward yellow tile, and I wondered if that was my body ridding itself of toxins, a kind of systemic gag-reaction to poison.

Then I was sleeping, and I was sleeping still more, and it was sleep and more sleep. This was knock-out sleep, restful sleep, fitful sleep, sleep to get away from everything, sleep to go into everything. Into dreams, into some ragged path to the unconscious.

Sleep was like rain, I thought. It came from the sky and went to the ground. It soaked everything. Sleep was powerful, more powerful than the conscious, physical world even, and without it no life was possible. Just like with rain.

I turned over, and the window was deeply shaded but not as dark. Maybe it was nine in the morning, or two in the afternoon or six at night. I didn't know or couldn't tell.

Then Suzanne was in the room, and she said, "You've been asleep awhile," and she was smiling. She said, "You must be hungry." Suddenly I was.

"There're sandwiches in the kitchen. Why don't you try one?"

When I stood up I was suddenly shivering, and my stomach felt like a fist.

The hallway was not brightly lit, but there were lots of closed doorways, and down to the left was the glassed-in nurse's station, which was brightly lit. The kitchen was to the right, and was not a large room. It had a table and chairs, a sink and microwave, a small refrigerator, baskets of fruit and pretzels and popcorn.

I thought I'd throw up, but took a sandwich and milk anyway, and sat down. Unwrapping the sandwich from the cellophane seemed to take a long time. My fingers were bouncing off the cellophane, and when I pressed a forefinger at what I thought was an opening I gouged a hole in the bread. My fingers were jumping, popping up from the smooth surface as though my hands were electrified.

My shoulder and leg were twitching too. Not constantly, but every half minute or minute. It seemed as though I'd lost control of my body.

I took a bite, chewed and swallowed, and felt like throwing up.

My shoulder jumped. I took a swig of milk, a small bite, another swig, then threw the sandwich away.

Was this withdrawal? I wondered. Then I thought, Was this detox? Was this eight milligrams of Ativan a day?

I dumped the milk in the sink, threw the empty carton away, went out to the hall, looked for my room. I didn't know what number it was, and I couldn't see numbers on any of the rooms.

Around the corner was another hallway, and a half stairway about sixty feet down. There were doors after doors after doors. There were name plates next to each one. James Conrad, Constance Winray, Edward Lucano. There was one for Financial Support and another for Computer Support, one for Institutional Planning, another for Physical Plant. Dawn Slovak had an office next to Walter Lennon.

Just past their offices, almost without noticing, I swayed, brushed the wall for a foot or two, then banged the wall, first with my shoulder, then lightly with my head.

I regained my balance, but swayed way over to the other side, and banged into a heavy wooden door with my shoulder, slid across the door and hit the metal door frame.

Leaning against the door, I stood up straight, but everything felt like a boat on turbulent water.

I tried to adjust my feet and legs, then told myself a few clonazepam or diazepam would steady and right the world.

I blinked, blinked some more, then pushed on past more doors, farther down the hall. The stairs were still a long way away, but past one more office door was a door with a glass window. Through the window there was another hallway. I pushed through the doorway, then thought I heard my name, paused, wasn't sure.

The closing door hit me on the arm and shoulder, and I stumbled against a wall. I heard my name again, more clearly this time, so I rested there.

A woman came through the door and almost fell over me. She was fairly young, no more than twenty-six, twenty-eight. She had a lovely face. Large green eyes, full lips, an aquiline nose, auburn hair gathered on top of her head and falling down the back of her neck.

She wore a brightly colored smock like the ones so many of the nurses wore, and then I noticed a nametag. She was Abigail Wyans R.N.

"You've wandered away, Paul," she said, and she looked amused.

"I kind of—" My voice disappeared.

"Got lost." She smiled. She had small, even teeth that were very white.

I nodded.

"So you wanna head back? You're due for your Ativan."

I was leaning, kind of slumping, down the wall.

She reached for my arm. "You need a hand?"

Her grip was strong.

We went back through the door, and began to walk. I brushed a wall, tried to right myself, and bumped Abigail. "God," I said, "Jesus. Sorry."

"Balance not so good?"

"It used to be pretty good. It's gotten kind of rocky."

"Maybe withdrawal. That can happen."

We were walking slowly, more slowly than I'd realized when I was alone.

Then I swayed toward her, and in trying to avoid her, I stumbled.

"I can't have you doing a header or a face plant. Honest."

Honest.

"I'll just hang on to your arm and we'll go slow."

Slowly we went. Somewhere in some expensive rehab in the hills of Pennsylvania, at some hour of the day or night. In this windowless warren of halls and doors and overhead lights.

"This is two days," I said.

"Two days what?"

"Since I've been here?"

"Ha."

I looked at her.

"Try four days plus."

Maybe the sleep did it, I thought. Drugs and detox. Time widened and narrowed, expanded and collapsed. Ten minutes became an hour, a day a week. Or the other way around.

When we finally got to the nurse's station, the two nurses behind the glass barely looked up.

Abigail went through the doorway at the back of the station to get my pills, came back with two tiny paper cups, one for pills, one for water, then took my blood pressure and pulse.

"What if you get no pulse?" I asked, just to see what she'd say.

"Send you to the morgue." She didn't smile.

"Abigail," I said, "you're too fast for me. You're lightning."

One other nurse was looking up. She had long black-gray hair pulled over one shoulder.

A woman my age shuffled past in the hall in slippers and a bathrobe. Her hair was wild, and she was breathing through her mouth. She stared at me as though it was me, and not her, who just arrived from another planet.

"Hi Rose," the quiet nurse said.

The woman in the robe said nothing. She went into the lounge and the door snapped shut behind her.

The watching nurse said, "Paul, you're going up to Men's Primary in about an hour. They'll be coming down for you. Okay?"

I said yes, and she said I could wait in the lounge, and they'd find me.

Sunlight was falling through the lounge windows, and another Mel Brooks movie was on, everyone in Robin Hood and Maid Marion outfits. The bad guys wore black. There was no sound.

Two young guys with long hair sat on one couch in the lounge. One was half asleep, the other was blond and friendly. He said his name was Chuck and he was in the Adolescent Unit, and detoxing, "from every fucking drug in the universe." He laughed. "I guess it's not funny," he added. "Especially for my mom and dad."

"No," I said, and I didn't know where that came from.

The woman with the wild hair and bathrobe looked up at me, then away, and I thought, God, my kids. My wife. What about them?

I thought of being back in my office, lying on my side on the futon, wanting so badly to be done. A plastic trash bag over my head, and cinched tight at my neck.

I could feel myself breathing inside the bag, could feel how little air there was, and how hot and moist and close it was. And told myself to be calm, to hold on, to stay in there.

And felt my bowels and bladder empty, and saw white dots on black, black dots on white.

I felt very cold, and trembled.

"You okay?" a woman said.

A woman with red hair.

She was in her forties, had a flat nose, and wore a pink fleece jacket.

Her hair was combed neatly to her shoulders, and she smiled as she sat. She didn't look as though she belonged here.

She was far too well put together, too composed. She looked like she was waiting for an airplane in New York or Chicago.

She looked over at me and said, "You're new." I said I came in a few days ago, and she said that's when she came in.

She had an even, confident voice, the voice of a teacher or public speaker. "I'm afraid I'm boring. I'm only here for wine. Wine and nothing else."

She smiled, seemed apologetic.

"Wine'll get you there. Wine'll get you where you need to go," I said.

She nodded, smiled more. She had a wonderful smile. Her nose was a boxer's bashed-in nose, but it gave her this curious, off-balance beauty.

"You?"

"Benzos."

She nodded. "Dalmane? Xanax? Temazepam? Clonazepam? Lorazepam?"

"How'd you know so many?"

"I'm a doctor."

"Wow."

"Yeah."

She smiled.

"Go ahead," she said. "Say things."

"Like?"

She shook her head.

I told her my name. Hers was Juliet.

"So we're the same day?" she said.

I nodded.

"I would've gone up sooner but my blood pressure was spiking," she said.

I looked at her.

I nodded again. She nodded.

The door opened and the nurse with hair down over one eye said, "Paul, your escorts are here." She smiled, and one of her front teeth was crooked.

"So long," I said to Juliet, and she said, "Nice to meet you."

There were two tall lean guys standing in the hall in front of the nurses' station. They were grinning, and they almost banged into me when they stepped forward to pump my hand. They grabbed each of my arms to steady me.

They were Alan and Levon.

"Welcome," they said.

Alan had short brown hair, blue eyes, and he stood very straight. His voice was deep, and his laugh was a jackhammer; it came from way down in his chest.

Alan wore flip flops, blue jeans, a blue fleece jacket.

He said, "Really, dude, it's great guys on Men's Primary. We take care of each other."

We had started through halls.

"I work for a tree company," he said. "Prune sick trees, work with ropes and chainsaw."

We went down halls, around corners, went right, went left, went past doors and through doors. Each time, one of them held the door, and either Levon or Alan put a hand on my back, asked how I was doing.

"How's the taper?" Levon asked, and I said, "I'm down to twelve milligrams of Ativan a day. I think."

They both laughed.

"You think," Levon said. Then he said, "How long you been here?"

"Three, four, five days. Something like that."

Levon was from New York City, he said. He managed a bar, drank and shot heroin.

We were still in halls, still among doors. There was a black sign on a wall with white lettering. It read, Founders, Atkins, Chit Chat, maybe something else. There were white arrows.

Levon wore long tan cargo shorts and a brown tee shirt, black sneakers, no socks. He was a guy you'd notice on a street. He was at least as tall as me and Alan. His dark hair was so short it looked as though it had been shaved a few days ago. He had a close-trimmed Fu Manchu mustache, and skinny legs, one of which had a long black tattoo that ran from near his knee to his ankle. It looked like an inverted L with a smaller, shadow L next to it.

We approached a door.

I could hear voices, laughter, more voices.

Guys.

"Welcome," Levon said.

He opened the door, and I could see a lounge beyond him, furniture, a fireplace, and the faces and figures of men. All kinds of men.

Alan said, "C'com, dude, they're friendly."

I heard Levon say, "Ladies, this is Paul."

And there was a crowd in front of me. Ten, fifteen, twenty guys. Shaking hands.

They said welcome. They said good luck.

4

A few of the men looked to be in their late twenties, one or two in their sixties or early seventies, but most were in their thirties or middle-aged. There were about twenty in all.

They wore shorts, jeans, chinos, tee-shirts, polo shirts, sweat-shirts, sweaters, sneakers, sandals. A few wore doo-rags, some had on baseball caps, one wore his turned sideways, and about a third of the guys had tattoos on their forearms. One guy was bald and had a flaming sun tattoo on the side of his skull.

They gathered around me, behind a big, dark blue couch, and took turns shaking my hand and introducing themselves. "Hey," they said. "Hi." "How you doing?" "They taking you down easy?" "Good to have you with us."

They were named Mick, Mike, Matty, Jeb, Rick, Ralph, Max, Rick, Mike, John, Carl, John, Matt, Chris, and other names too. Lots of other names. I thought the Mike Mike and Rick Rick and John John might be some kind of joke or trick or test. Then there was a Bert with a powerful Southern accent. He was a few inches shorter than me, with a huge head of bright white hair, so white it was almost blue, and a big white, cartoon-like mustache. Like a sheriff or politician or golfer.

I asked where he was from, and he said Tennessee, and I told him that was where my wife was from.

"Where bouts?" he asked.

"The east, near Knoxville."

"Oh I'm way the hell out West. Memphis. Near the river."

I nodded.

"You lemme know, we'll go burn one," he said.

"What?"

"Burn one. Have a smoke." He cackled. "You still fucked up on them pills. Man, you're dumb as shit."

We both started laughing.

The lounge was the size of a large living room. There was a fireplace on one wall, and next to that a very long hall. Two big blue couches and three large easy chairs, two tables behind one couch. There was a galley kitchen, what looked like a staff office, a laundry room, a wall of windows with a glass door in the middle, and out the door a narrow patio with Adirondack chairs.

"What'd you say your name was?" I asked the white-haired guy.

"Bert, with an *e*. Not a *u*."

He had a big belly. He wore tan shorts, and had thick, hairless legs. Bert looked almost pregnant.

"I'll write it down," I said.

He chuckled. "You do that, motherfucker. Least you know how to write." He looked me up, he looked me down. "You know something?"

"What's that?"

"I asked staff how old you were," Bert said. He coughed, a deep, three packs a day cough. "I'm younger than you."

There were broken blood vessels in his face, pouches under his eyes, and he could have been pushing seventy.

"Nah," I said.

"I'm fifty-two."

"Scary."

"Tell me about it."

"What'd you drink? Drano?"

Bert laughed more, and it sounded like his lungs were coming up.

We both looked across the room. Two guys sat on one couch, one sat on another. A guy sat on a big chair. The guy in the chair had a shaved head and an earring in each ear.

Bert said, "You want I show you around. You wanna go burn one?"

"Paul," I heard, and Bert said, "That motherfucking junky."

Levon. He was coming down the long long hall with a guy wearing a bright bow tie.

I looked at Bert.

"Don't you know I'm just shitting you, professor? You dumb fuck. Levon is one great fucking guy."

We both turned, and Levon said, "Guys."

"Gentlemen," the bow tie man said. "Hello."

"Hey Bowtie," Bert said.

"Bow Tie," Levon said.

"Paul, I'm Ed Wharton, otherwise known as Bow Tie, one of the counselors on the Unit." He shook my hand.

"Don't fuck with Bow Tie," Bert said, "even though he looks like some Yankee pussy." He chuckled his three packs a day chuckle. "He's a tenth degree black belt in that Chinese shit."

"Aikido?" Levon said. "Karate?"

"Second degree," Bow Tie said. "Aikido."

He wore a pink Oxford shirt, and his big bow tie had more color than the tail of a peacock. He had round wire-rim glasses, a blond crewcut, full red lips, a small nose. He was shorter than the three of us, but stood tall, like a dancer at rest. His torso was powerful under the pink shirt. He had big shoulders that sloped to his upper arms.

"How you doing, Paul?" he said. "They showing you around?"

I nodded.

"The withdrawal okay?" he asked.

"So far."

Doors on all sides of the room opened and closed, slammed, slapped, banged.

"Dude," someone said loud. Someone else said, "Hey."

I noticed, I guess for the first time, that all patients were wearing red wrist bracelets, and staff had ID cards around their necks, hung by cords, or clipped to pockets. I looked down at mine on my right wrist. It said, Cody, P. E mycin. That was an antibiotic I was allergic to.

A very tall guy with a long gray ponytail came up to us. He was Max, and he was wearing a ratty tan sportscoat with loose threads at the elbows and pockets. He moved as he stood like a dealer on a street corner. Everything shifted, jerked, bounced. His eyes worked over the room.

Max said he'd show me around. Bowtie said if I needed anything to shout, Bert said he was gonna burn one, Levon said he would too. So Max took me down the long hall, past dozens of doors, and he said, "You really a writer?" And I said I was. He said he was too.

I asked what he wrote, and he said he was from New York City.

"What?" I asked.

"Chelsea," he said.

"What do you write?" I asked. "You said you write."

We went through a glass door at the end of the hall, into a lobby. Outside double glass doors there was a bell tower, then across a small road there was a gazebo. Next to the gazebo there were maybe eight or ten Adirondack chairs and a bench. Guys were smoking cigarettes like they were about to be executed, like this was the last best thing they'd ever tasted.

In the other direction, through the lobby, there was an auditorium. Chit Chat Auditorium, said a sign.

"Fucking Meth," Max said. "Fucking crank and crack."

I looked down and noticed how thin his wrists were. Sapling wrists. So skinny they looked like they'd snap. And his teeth were yellow and very long, the gums receded almost to the bones of his jaw.

"You do meth?" he asked. "You do crack?" His eyes seemed almost metallic.

"Some pain pills, mostly benzos."

His eyes flickered. A spark in the deep circuit. Interstellar.

"Benzos are underrated," Max said. "Valium's got you covered, whatever you need. Temazepam. Dalmane." He looked me long in the eyes.

Maybe Max wasn't so crazy. He knew about temazepam, which almost nobody heard about, except Julie with the pink jacket, but she was a doctor. And Dalmane, the old sleeping pill from the 1970's. Almost no one knew about that, except me and Julie of course. And Max.

"You get them from a doc? Doctor Feelgood?"

His eyes were glistening.

"Web sites."

He kept looking at me with those shining eyes. I stared at my feet. My Danskos looked like Dutch clogs. I thought, My Danskos are Dutch clogs.

"You wanna give Max those web addresses?"

I knew it was coming. I could see this a long way off.

"My memory's shot, Max. I can't remember my own email address."

"Fucking crank," he said. "Fucking crack." He looked at me closely and carefully. "Do them, my friend. Do them and we'll see where your memory be."

His eyes frosted over. I couldn't tell where or how he was. The only genuine moments with Max seemed to be when he mentioned temazepam and Dalmane, and asked for drug web addresses.

"So anything else you wanna see, dude?" he asked.

I almost laughed. We hadn't seen anything. A long hallway, a doorway, a lobby.

"What's that?" I said, pointing at the auditorium.

We walked toward the closed double doors, and big glass panels on each side of the doors. Inside, there were rows of red seats, a podium, windows and doors on the sides.

"You spend half your life there," Max said. "Lectures, meetings, talks, almost everything. They keep the air conditioning on full blast all the time so nobody falls asleep. So bring your sweater and coat. You hear me. Otherwise you catch bronchitis. Then you catch pneumonia. And they don't give you codeine cough syrup here at Caron. Not a chance."

I laughed.

"You seem to know the drill, Max."

"Fuck, yes."

"How long you been in?"

"Week."

"Just a week?"

"I was in the hospital three weeks before that. Intensive care."

"For what?"

"Everything. Lungs, veins, heart, brain. Life by a thread. You know what I'm saying."

"You almost checked out?"

His skin was yellow. Same with the whites of his eyes. There were bruises on the backs of his hands, but I had assumed that was from his own needles. Maybe they were from hospital sticks.

"Shit, yeah. I was out of there. I was gone already."

"Except you weren't."

"Correct."

I looked at him for a while, and he looked at the floor or at his shoes or at something. I couldn't tell.

"There," he said, and pointed over my shoulder, at the wall opposite the auditorium doors.

There were panels hung on the wall, and attached to the panels were hundreds and hundreds of flat metal tags. They were about two by five inches, and they had names etched into them, and were arranged according to how much money they had donated to Caron.

At the bottom, near the floor, were the five thousand dollar donors, then moving up to ten, twenty-five, fifty, one hundred thousand, finally to the five hundred thousand and million dollar range. Liza Minnelli, Matt Dillon and Matthew Broderick were way up near the top. Aerosmith was at the top and so was Coors Beer.

"Some shit," Max said. I could feel his breath on my neck. It did not feel or smell healthy.

He smelled like a room that had been closed for weeks and even months. The bed or couch, the drapes and rugs and pillows, had not been exposed to light or air in a long time. Then with a shiver, I thought of the upholstery, the lining, in a buried coffin.

I turned fast, and the benzo swoosh thing happened. My body, my head, were a foot faster than my eyes and my brain. I staggered and almost went to the floor.

Max was only a foot away from me, and I wanted to get away from him.

His long teeth, long hair, the scarecrow sportscoat flapping around his upper body, the caved-in cheeks, the almost dead eyes that looked at you or through you, or at someone twenty years ago.

There in the lobby, and I looked back at him, and I saw my face those times when I was really messed up and looked in a mirror. Those awful times when I was late in a bad run. And I might be twenty years old or forty-nine. I'd turn, and see that other person looking at me. His face was tissue white, his eyes flat, and he was very old. He had lost everything vital. He had no soul. I was a thread away from Max.

I turned and saw another person looking at me. More than forty years ago, in Newton, Massachusetts, the city where I grew up. I was thirteen, in ninth grade, and my girlfriend, Helen, and I were standing in the bathroom off her parents' bedroom, looking through the medicine cabinet.

Helen's house was a wonder to me, an enormous split-level with at least five big bedrooms, three or four bathrooms, a maid's quarters, a sauna, everything. And they just had two kids. My family had one bathroom for seven people, and we didn't even have a car.

Maybe that's why Helen and I were so in love: the upper middle class Jewish girl and the working class Irish Catholic boy. Plus we both loved pharmaceuticals.

The medicine cabinet was loaded with amber drug vials. We more or less knew what to look for from reading the anti-drug pamphlets they handed out in school. The pamphlets had descriptions of what the pills were for, and how they made you feel. Just about anything that treated pain, anxiety or sleeplessness could get you high. The pamphlets even had photographs of many of the pills.

I sat on the edge of the bathtub, the shower curtain draped over me like a cape, and I thought, We're about to fly. The shower curtain was tan and matched the rug, the toilet seat cover and the window curtains.

Helen handed me a pill bottle. Big fat pills. Something-icin. Take three times a days. It sounded like medicine for an infection.

I shook my head.

"No?" Helen said. She was no more than five feet tall, she was almost a year older than me, nearly fourteen, and she had a woman's body.

"Here," she said, and handed me another bottle. Take one two times a day for seizure. Phenobarbital, 60 m.g. Yes.

"Helen," I said. "Oh boy."

There had to have been at least a hundred tiny white phenobarbital tablets.

"What?"

"A wicked good pill, and a whole bunch of them."

They were prescribed to Helen's dad, a Harvard engineering grad, who owned a company that manufactured parts that went into rocket engines. Or something like that. He was a rocket scientist.

He was a thin bald guy who was always nice to me.

He also had codeine. Take one or two for pain every four to six hours.

Helen's mother had Seconal for sleep and Valium for anxiety.

The house was utterly silent around us. There was no dripping water or clanking radiators the way there were at my house. There was no traffic passing out front, no cars and trucks, no kids shouting in the neighborhood.

Helen's mom and dad were away for the weekend.

We each took five phenobarbital, two codeine, and two Seconal and Valium. I put the pills in the watch pocket of my jeans, Helen put hers in a small plastic container that used to hold breath mints.

She plucked out a yellow Valium, I fished a codeine, a phenobarbital and a Valium from my jeans. Helen poured us a cup of water, handed it to me, and I put the three pills in the back of my mouth, swallowed, chased it with water. Helen took the Valium.

We put the pill bottles back in the cabinet, made sure everything looked right, then shut the light off. Back in the den, Helen asked me what I wanted to do. I looked at her.

"Hang out here, or go walk around?"

If we went out to walk we could get pulled over by the cops, and maybe searched, but cops didn't do that much in Newton, especially in neighborhoods like this. That might happen, but it wasn't very likely to happen.

So there Helen and I were, on a mid-May evening, on the streets of this upper-middle class neighborhood, walking slowly, holding hands, going past big handsome houses and flowering fruit trees with delicate pink and peach flowers. Then the pills were kicking in, and any pain or anxiety was gone. It was vapor, and the two of us were floating. We were painless and happy, and it seemed as though we would be like that forever.

"Dude," Max said.

"What?"

"Let's head back to the lounge."

Outside the double glass doors, the gazebo was deserted.

"Where is everybody?"

"Meeting. There's meetings and lectures and shit all the time."

He opened the door to the long hallway. It was empty, as though someone had opened a can of nerve gas.

I walked behind him. He took long strides, but they were uneven. They'd go from one side of the hall to the other. Then I realized that mine did too.

I tried to walk straight, to keep each footstep in the middle of the hallway. I did it for one or two steps. Then the third step went off to the right. The fourth to the left, the fifth way over to the right, the sixth very far over.

We reached the lounge and there was nobody there.

5

I wandered over to the kitchen, to a sink, a counter, a coffee machine, a juice machine, and a small refrigerator under the counter. I checked out a basket of fruit with apples, pears, oranges, bananas, and a basket with small packages of pretzels and popcorn.

On the opposite wall I saw a narrow table of forms. I found a stack of sheets, Primary Care Men—Patient Schedule. From Monday through Sunday, 6:30 in the morning until Lights Out at 11:00 p.m., something was scheduled almost all the time. Breakfast at seven, lunch at 11:30, dinner at 5:00.

I wasn't sure what day it was. I checked my watch. It was blinking, which meant it was in SET mode. I had probably rolled over it while sleeping.

I looked for Max, but he'd slipped away as suddenly as he'd appeared. I took the schedule, and sat on the end of one of the couches.

Monday morning: Wake Up; Breakfast; Medication; Meditation; Lecture; Unit Group; Medication; Lunch. That looked pretty busy.

The place was awfully silent, especially considering twenty or thirty guys lived here, and another fifteen or twenty people worked here. There were a few copies of the AA big books on the coffee table, some sections of newspapers, three Styrofoam cups, an empty popcorn bag, a pen on top of a partially completed crossword puzzle.

I was feeling twitchy again. There were moments when I felt as though I'd have to stand up and run to get out of myself, out of my skin. Or as if I simply wouldn't be able to stand the way I felt. This intensely raw, uncomfortable feeling, this generalized itch, this need to scream, had spread to every part of me.

So I sat in the lounge of Founder's Hall, in Men's Primary at Caron Treatment Center, where I imagined many thousands of people must have felt this way over the years and decades.

Then I heard footsteps and the big door behind me pushed open, banged shut, and a short guy came through with my black bag over his shoulder. He was rattling a bunch of keys, and bristling with energy. He said, "Hey, I'm Dave, a CA, a Counselor's Assistant. I've got your bag."

He stood in front of me and shook my hand before I could stand up. I tried to stand up, but sat back by the time he had turned away and was fumbling for a key to the office door.

I made it up on the third try.

"How you doing?" he called to me.

"Pretty good," I said. "I just found a schedule."

"Yeah, you'll get caught up with that pretty quick. It takes a few days, especially after detox."

"I'm still catching up with myself."

"Well the nice thing working here is that we see people catch up, and that's good."

"You do see it?"

Dave had opened the door and gone inside the office. I stayed on the couch. I heard a computer start up, keys jangle, a window open.

Dave came to the office door. "We do see it," he said.

I almost said, "Huh?" Time kept happening in this slowed-down then sped-up way. You'd ask a question, then three minutes later you might get half an answer.

Dave looked at me as though I had said something. He was in his mid forties, had short hair, thinning on top. He wore a short-sleeved dress shirt, gray dress pants, and had a mess of keys on his belt.

"I'll show you your room, and we'll go through your luggage. That's a rule here in case you wanted to bring in a bottle of booze or some pills or whatever."

"I understand."

"Or maybe you forgot you brought it in or left it in your bag." He smiled a lopsided smile. "Hard to tell sometimes. Know what I mean?"

I didn't say anything. I wasn't sure. Maybe.

He went from the doorway back into the office, then came back with my bag.

"Wanna see your room, go through your bag?"

I got up on the first try, and followed him. It was the first room on the right on the long hall, next to the lounge.

Inside, it was pretty small. Two beds, one dresser, a tiny desk, a wardrobe. There was a small bathroom, a big window over the bed on the far wall. Dave pointed to that bed and said it would be mine.

"You'll have your own room for a night or two, but we're starting to fill up. You should get a roommate by Thursday or Friday.'

"Is today Wednesday?"

He paused. He seemed to think I was joking.

"My watch is messed-up. I don't remember how to set it." I held my wrist out with the watch blinking. "I used to know," I said.

"Take it off. Lemme see if I can help."

I handed it to him. He dropped the bag next to the bed, sat down, and said, "Have a seat." I thought twice. I thought three times.

Then I sat down next to him, at least a foot away.

The bed was firm and small. My legs were banging into my bag. This seemed like a dorm room.

There were a series of beeps, and the face of my watch lit up. "Okay," Dave said. "There we go." A few more beeps. "So that's it. Hmmm."

"It's 4:11, Wednesday afternoon, May 20."

I looked at the face of the watch, which was no longer blinking. The time, day and date were as Dave said.

"As far as the schedule goes, everyone's at gym. That's from 3:30 to 4:30. Then dinner's at five. That's down the road at the cafeteria. Some of the guys will show you." He looked at me and smiled. "Not Max," he said. "Between you and me. He has a pretty heavy detox. You go with him and you may end up in downtown Wernersville."

I nodded.

"So let's go through your bag."

He leaned over, unzipped the bag, and started fishing through my stuff. Boxers, socks, one pair of jeans, a sweater, tee-shirts, a raincoat, two books on Buddhism. Only books on spirituality were allowed. Then toiletries.

The Caron website had said that no guns, knives, alcohol, or drugs were allowed. I laughed hard when I read that. Now I wouldn't laugh.

"You one of us, Dave?"

"Oh yeah. Definitely."

He'd been sober eighteen years.

I looked at him. He had a square jaw. He was clean-shaven.

Once upon a time, in what seemed almost a fairy tale, I had twenty-five years. I had a quarter century clean and sober.

Between the ages of twenty-three and forty-eight, I didn't take an illicit drug or a single drink of alcohol. Then I did.

Dave said everything looked good. He said I'd have the top three drawers in the dresser, and half the wardrobe. He said the guys would be coming back from the gym in half an hour.

"If you wanna have a smoke, the Butt Hut's right across the road, out the door from the kitchen."

There was a patio out the kitchen door, a small lawn, and a winding path, which I followed. Then a small road for service vehicles and a gazebo across the road. Next to it were about ten Adirondack chairs and a bench set on gravel, facing the woods.

Nobody was there.

I sat down on the bench, lit a Kool, and stared up through trees. This was the first smoke I'd had in I didn't know how long. It tasted good. The smoke rose, held together for a moment, then swirled wildly toward the sky.

I thought of Liz and Liam and Austin, 222 miles away. Going to school, work, running, singing, hanging out with friends.

Liz had a slight southern accent that became more pronounced when she spoke on the phone with her mother, who was in Knoxville, Tennessee. Will became wiiii-illl, sure was shuu-urrre.

We lived in a house that was almost a hundred years old. It was a beater when Liz and I bought it, with fake wood paneling on the walls, an old kitchen and a single rusting bathroom. Our neighborhood, Fall Creek, was only a half mile to downtown Ithaca and a half mile to Cornell's Arts Quad. Most of the houses were student rentals, and that meant loud parties most weekends, couches and empty beer kegs on front porches.

In the nearly twenty years we'd lived there both the neighborhood and our house changed. Many of the students were gone. The few who remained were graduate students. The houses were mainly bought up by young families.

Houses got painted, there were often contractors' vans parked on the streets, we'd see young pony-tailed moms pushing strollers, and there were neighborhood picnics. Before long, it seemed, we actually knew our neighbors.

We had first one son, a redhead, then three years later, a second son, another redhead.

Year by year, we had windows replaced, paneling removed, wiring and floors redone, rooms and heat added. The attic turned into an office; the bathroom was gutted and a second one constructed. There was a new dining room in back, with bare oak and windows that looked onto the trees in the back yard. When the river birch and dogwood turned orange and yellow, and we watched it from the dinner table, our world seemed perfect.

Sitting in a chair at the Butt Hut I thought of Liz, in 1987, reading from her first published book of poems, *The Patience of the Cloud Photographer,* at a bookstore in Ithaca. The poem was called "To the Reservoir."

> If I walked the long way around
> to the reservoir maybe I would know
> pain. In the course of the walk the sky
> might go smoky and impotent, the dark
> leaves tired of their weight, decked
> for pain's progress.

The collection came out in 1987, but the poem was written well before Liam, our oldest, was born. The whole thing, more than twenty hours of back labor followed by a C-section, was an astonishment, a shock, a sustained, breathtaking dunk in ice water.

The fact that Liz was willing to do it again less than three years later says much about the glorious charm of children.

Years later, in the seventh grade, Liam was reading Shakespeare for English class. Liam's class was reading *Twelfth Night,* which begins, "If music be the food of love, play on."

He was fascinated by the clown, Feste, and he came up to my office to talk.

Feste, he said, was so fast and smart and he was just a clown. He could talk rings around anybody. He could insult them, call them names, goof on them, tell jokes, do anything, and half the time they didn't even know.

"What else?" I asked. "Something you can always count on from Shakespeare's clowns."

Liam looked at me.

His hair was red, and came down nearly to his chin. His nose was thin, his eyes blue. He was wearing a grey flannel shirt nearly worn through at the elbows.

"He always says…" he began.

"Says?"

We were surrounded by shelves and shelves of books. Hundreds and hundreds of books. A thousand books. Two thousand books. There was a print of a blue Klee boat on the wall, with red and yellow flags flying from it.

Liam pushed his hair behind his ears. He sat back in his chair, then leaned forward on his knees. A few cars passed on the street out front.

"Feste always says what people are afraid to say, or what they don't see," Liam said.

"He always says the truth."

He looked up fast. He stared hard at me. "He always tells the truth."

A spring breeze outside the window pushed leaves through the oak tree in the night air.

An Adirondack chair creaked, and I looked over. There was a man who was maybe thirty, sitting, smiling, lighting a cigarette, and another guy about my age who was standing near the front of the gazebo, smoking. The second guy had a crewcut, a cut that soldiers called "high and tight," and he wore a brown leather jacket.

The smiling man stood up, came over and said, "How you doing?" He shook my hand. "Hey," he said.

I told him my name and he said he'd met me earlier. His name was Ricky. I had no memory of him at all.

"How's your detox?" he said.

I said that as far as I could tell they were bringing me down pretty gently.

"All fucked up," a voice said. The voice was slow, sounded like it came from the trees or the gazebo.

I looked over and the guy with the crew cut was blowing smoke toward the clock tower.

"That's Tim," Ricky said. "Hey, Tim, say hello to Paul."

"All fucked up," Tim said, and it was the same voice. Tim was looking at the bell tower.

"Tim doesn't say much," Ricky whispered.

"Right," Tim said.

Ricky and I looked at each other. Then Ricky said, "Tim was in Vietnam. And he doesn't talk much, and he loves to drink. That's all I know."

"Fucking right," Tim said. "All you need to know."

I lit another Kool, and the three of us smoked quietly. The leaves stirred softly overhead, and a motor—maybe a lawnmower—started up way off in the distance.

My eyes were closed, and I pictured my younger son, Austin, who turned thirteen a few weeks before I came here. A few days before his birthday he had a well visit with his pediatrician, and when the nurse weighed and measured him she was astonished. He had grown six inches the previous year, from five-one to five-seven. He'd gone from a boy to a young man. His voice had changed. He was way taller than his mother. If he grew according to the charts, his doctor said, and these were hardly scientific, she added, he could be anywhere between six-two and six-five.

"You need a smoke?" Ricky asked, and I shook my head, said thanks.

I lit another, leaned back, and tried to remember how long I'd been at Caron. A week? Close to a week? Somewhere around there. I wasn't sure. This was the first time I had thought of Liam and Austin in that time.

This was the longest I had been away from them. Ever.

But when I was home in my office on the third floor, hour after hour, day after day, almost never coming down except to use the bathroom or to check the mail, what was that?

Did that count as a long time away?

The plastic bag had been over my head for several minutes. It was hot and wet, and I couldn't breathe. The spots in front of my eyes were black and white and white and black. Another thirty seconds, I thought, and I'd be unconscious.

I pictured Austin's face. His curly red hair, his smile, his eyes.

I reached up, grabbed the plastic, ripped it.

Felt cool, cool air, rich air, abundant air. I breathed fast, then slowly and deeply. Breathed again, and breathed deeper. Breathed more and more and more.

6

Marcel was showing me the way to the cafeteria, telling me how much he hated Caron. How much it sucked, big-time, sucked more than I could imagine, sucked like grade school sucked, and he meant grade school with the fucking nuns in those penguin outfits, the ones who banged you across the knuckles with the big wooden rulers.

"You know what I mean?" he said.

Marcel was short, smoked menthols like me, wore a gray tee-shirt, jeans, sandals, a Rolex, was a graphic designer, was married with two small kids, and lived in a gated community in Ottawa. That was in Canada. Ya know. A lot of fucking people in this country didn't know. They thought Ottawa was a county in Wyoming or in fucking Idaho for the love of God. At least he knew Idaho and Wyoming were states in the States if I knew what he meant.

"Do you?" he asked. Marcel didn't wait for an answer.

He got in trouble with Klonopin, one of my principal drugs of trouble and choice, and when we learned that we both used Klonopin we laughed and actually hugged.

He spoke slow and low.

We walked along the small road, between the very long, low building and the woods. There was another, smaller gazebo, and this, Marcel said, was where the women smoked. We must never speak to the women, he said, not ever, not even for a minute.

"Where are they?" I asked.

"Somewhere in there." He indicated with his cigarette the low building.

"What else is in there?"

"Fuck if I know." He started laughing.

Then Marcel was telling me how he got to Caron. He was home in the middle of the afternoon arguing with his wife. About his use of clonnies. What else? His wife sent the nanny upstairs with the kids. Then they really started hollering. Thank God there were no neighbors within a few hundred yards.

So Marcel was pretty looped on Klonopin. The argument moved outside to the front porch. He was so frustrated with his wife, and he was so fucked-up on maybe ten or fifteen clonnies that he whipped out his cell phone and called the cops.

I said, "Excuse me?"

"What?"

"You did what?"

"I called the cops."

"What exactly did you have in mind?"

"They were gonna arrest my wife."

"On what grounds?"

"Being unreasonable."

"Is that a felony in Canada?"

"Fuck you, Professor."

"No offense, dude—"

"I'm sick of the fucking Canadian jokes."

"Marcel, does this sound like a good idea? Calling the cops when you're jacked on benzos?"

"It gets better."

"I can't wait."

So the cops arrived pretty quickly. This was a gated community. Two big cops came up to the front porch, and Marcel ordered them to arrest his wife. They said no. His wife told the cops her husband was on drugs, which was evident anyway. They tried to calm Marcel, but he was outraged that they wouldn't arrest his wife. He screamed, they put their hands on his shoulders to quiet him, he shoved them, they shoved back, he went for one of their guns and didn't get it.

Marcel ended up in handcuffs, face down on the deck of the porch, then face down in the back seat of the police car. Marcel ended up in jail for about a week. The only reason he didn't end up in jail longer was that he was arrested under Canada's Mental Health Act, which meant that he was arrested not as a felon but as a crazy person.

"They let me come here for thirty-one days instead of staying in jail."

"How was jail?"

"Fuck. If you think this fucking sucks, forget it."

We crested a hill on the small road, and there was a view of small mountains and farms, roads and lakes, that must have extended ten or fifteen miles. I could feel my lungs expand.

We had reached the end of the mile-long building, with several pauses along the road. Pauses where we stood in the middle of the road hooting and hollering while groups of people walked by. The building was more like an eighth of a mile long, a ranch house on steroids. There was a gap of fifty or a hundred feet, then a gorgeous, huge stone house with a belvedere on top.

Marcel didn't know what was in the stone house. But since the mention of jail I'd begun to feel weird. Had begun to feel withdrawal kick up. The odd, scary feeling, thoughts of going to jail because of all the pills in my possession, the pills I had taken, and all my large and small breaches of trust.

My kids asking me to watch a movie or play catch, and me saying I was too tired, I had to lie down. And sleeping when I should have been mowing the lawn, talking to my wife, eating dinner with the family, taking out the trash, being present. There were hundreds of small crimes. There were thousands.

And I thought of the thirty- and forty-foot walls of Auburn Correctional Facility, where I used to teach, walls topped by concertina wire, and guard towers with corrections officers holding high-powered rifles.

To get in we were searched, went into a glass and steel box, were counted, came out the far side of the box. We went up stairs, down a hall, past a checkpoint, through an enormous steel door. Then down a hall, through a door, down stairs, into another box. We were counted again, and went out a different side of the box.

Then we could see the huge cellblocks looming on the right, hear the trapped human noise, the shouts, whistles, singing, the cellblocks stacked like cages inside the building.

We walked along the building, and a twenty-five foot high fence, a gate you could drive a tank through, was up ahead. Beyond was the yard, empty at the moment, but surrounded by cellblocks, bare as a parking lot at two a.m., but lit like the sun itself.

The guards unlocked the gates, and once they let us into the bare light of the yard, the cellblocks went nuts.

"Fresh meat," they yelled.

"Honkey motherfucker."

"Rapo."

"Bend over."

The walk to the far side of the empty yard seemed to take a full day.

The Pennsylvania countryside was spectacular. Verdant, heavily wooded, patches of smooth green and brown where farmers had fields under cultivation.

Standing with Marcel, though, my hands, arms, and now my whole body was shaking. My shoulder was twitching, jumping, and my toes felt tingly, as though they were very cold.

"Dude," Marcel said. "Motherfucker."

I turned, and my head bobbed like a toy in the back window of a car.

"The fuck." He pulled on his cigarette. "What the. God."

"Drugs," I said.

"You get your detox med?"

"Where?"

"Where the fuck you think you get your detox med? Where you get your car fixed? The ice cream store?"

I looked at him, my head still bobbing.

"In detox, dude, the other end of the building."

I nodded, said thanks, turned.

The trees were big, and leaves moved constantly even though there was no wind.

Then I watched my shoes hit the pavement. My Dutch boy shoes.

And now they were hitting the ground. One, then the other one. Nerves in my legs and hips and feet were electric.

The hill went up and up. Then near a long flowerbed, under a line of tall pine trees, the hill started to go down. It went down gently at first, near the small gazebo, then it went a bit more steeply.

Slowly, then more slowly, watching my wobbly legs, my Dutch feet, I went down the hill as it got steep then steeper. People passed, and some said hello.

I went along the road between giant bushes that were at least fifteen feet tall and woods on the opposite side. Then I came to a small patio with a picnic bench and a door beyond it. Inside were more of those hallways, only now I asked a nurse, a woman in a brightly colored smock, how to get to detox.

She pointed, and there were the glass windows. I could feel every tremor in my body. I could feel muscles and nerves I had never known were there.

When the med nurse, the smiling short blond named Suzanne, handed me the small white cup with the pill, I asked how much.

"One milligram."

"Ouch."

She smiled.

"One tiny milligram."

She kept smiling.

On my way out, the picnic table was in the same place, and beyond that was the road and the woods. I figured if I walked far enough down the road I'd find the cafeteria, but I wasn't hungry.

About fifty feet uphill, there was a patch of grass between the road and the woods. I started walking in the grass, which felt soft, and I was walking under a canopy of branches and leaves.

About halfway between the detox and Butt Hut I sat down, and looked at the woods. They were thick as forest, and rose from below a small cliff that dropped sharply away.

It was almost all maple, with the occasional oak, aspen, walnut and pine. Light played on the leaves and trunks and branches, shifting constantly, forming beads and shards and shafts of light. It was dim, jeweled, dancing, fine.

I waited for the pill to kick in. One milligram was such a pathetically small amount that I couldn't believe all my hope resided in one pale Ativan.

There were so many times when I sat in my office with a handful of aluminum strips of two-milligram Ativan, each strip containing ten pills. I'd have fifty or a hundred in my hand, and these weren't even the strongest I had.

Hidden in my bookcases I'd have another two hundred Valium and two hundred Klonipin. The Ativan were like beer to whiskey.

The shocking thing was that I could feel it—slightly, just taking the very edge of an edge off.

Maybe it had to do with sitting on the grass, staring at the trees, watching light. Maybe it had to do with sitting alone.

I found a cigarette, lit it, watched the smoke rise, thought of tearing the bag off my head, going downstairs, taking a shower, throwing my soiled clothes outside in the trash, and later telling Liz what I had done.

"God," she had said, "God," and we talked for hours, and she took me finally to the Emergency Room, where I talked a psychiatrist out of admitting me to the psychiatric unit.

It was the booze, I had told him. Booze made me want to die. And I had to teach, anyway, I said. I had to finish the semester.

People walked by behind me. Fucking this, fucking that, they said.

They had to be patients.

I was a patient.

Old as I was, I was a patient.

Fifty-five years old.

College teacher.

Husband of Liz.

Father of Austin and Liam.

My name is Paul and I'm an alcoholic and addict.

I spotted blue jays on the branch of an oak. They stayed five seconds, then flitted away.

For the first time since I'd been here, I had the powerful desire to be elsewhere. I didn't know where elsewhere was. The only thing that was going to make me feel better right now was drugs.

But that was only going to prolong what I was going through right now.

But if I could do it right. Could use drugs right. Could get it right. Could drink right.

Use drugs and drink the way normal people did. Take a few pills, have a few drinks, get a little high, and then stop. Be a regular human being.

On the grass at Caron, I knew it was a lie, the big lie of my life. I'd known it, most of me had known it, for forty years.

I wasn't a regular human being, not when it came to alcohol and drugs.

For me, booze or drugs were love and warmth, air and water. They were necessary and essential. I could no more stop with one drink or drug than I could with one bite of food, one sip of water.

The light in the woods kept moving. There were more birds in the branches, more squirrels. The squirrels were amazingly fast, shockingly agile.

When was the last time I had marveled at nature, had thought about it at all? The last time I thought about anything?

More people walked by. They said hey. They said, How you doing.

Lower down the hill, to the left, past the detox, there was a parking lot, a road. Then up a steep hill on the other side there was a spectacular gray stone building that looked like a hotel or spa from a hundred years ago. It was flanked by two glassy new buildings, the ones I had noticed driving in.

Somehow, these people seemed less smashed-up than the people on this side of the road, in Primary and Relapse. Their eyes seemed more clear, and there was more spring in their step.

Up the hill, the Butt Hut was now crowded. Alan and Levon, the Vietnam guy, Marcel, Bert, Ricky, people I had met but whose names I couldn't remember. There had to be fifteen or twenty people, sitting, standing, smoking. There were shouts, hoots, gales of laughter. It looked like an aging, sloppy fraternity, only with far more tattoos.

I watched the woods some more. The light was lambent, and the birds and squirrels seemed to be multiplying. They weren't moving quite as quickly though, maybe because of the light. Or maybe that was me. Maybe I was less nervous.

Then it occurred to me that ten or twenty minutes ago, heading down the hill to detox, I had been worried about my ability to walk. And just by sitting, breathing, staring at light, trees, birds and squirrels, I had grown calm. Wasn't that kind of like meditation?

But then I thought, wasn't that kind of like one milligram of Ativan?

Whenever I read Eastern or Buddhist writings, even in a haphazard way, I felt calm. When I read in the Tao Te Ching, "If you want to know me, look into your heart," my mind could circle around and around that line for hours, until it became like listening to the beat of my heart. I'd grow quiet. Find what T.S. Eliot called "The still point in the turning world."

People were no longer passing on the small road, but the crowd at the Butt Hut had grown. There had to be thirty guys there.

I thought of Liz, Liam and Austin at home, and wondered what they were doing. Coming home from work, school, track and chorus practice. Liz in shorts, a black top, her long runner's legs pale, pulling weeds from a flower bed.

It was late May and the trees in the backyard were coming into full flower and leaf. In the last twenty years, we had planted an oak, a river birch, a European beech, a Chinese dogwood, a Bradford pear, a dogwood, a snakebark maple, a plum tree.

I was still watching the woods when I heard someone. "Dude. Hey, dude."

I didn't look up.

Then he was real close. He was very loud.

"Dude, hey."

I looked up, and there was a guy. A big guy. A huge guy.

"You okay?" he asked, in this rumbling voice.

I looked away and then back at him. He was immense. Six-five, easily. And he must have weighed at least two sixty or more.

His head was enormous, and he had a big Irish face. His hair was a mass of brown red curls tumbling to his shoulders.

"I'm Jake," he said.

He wore a tank top, shorts and sandals, and his arms and shoulders, chest and legs were layered with muscle. Even the tops of his toes were callused.

"Jake," I said.

He nodded. His eyes were friendly and warm.

"You're one of the biggest motherfuckers I've ever seen," I said. "And you've got calluses on your toes, for god's sake."

He laughed. "I'm a mixed martial artists fighter."

"Heavyweight?"

"How could you tell?"

We both laughed and then I got up and we walked to the Butt Hut.

Jake had played football in high school and then at a Division I college, before dropping out.

"And you're a writer, right?" he said.

I nodded. "Was."

He looked over at me for a while.

"I guess that's right about all of us."

"What?"

"None of us is."

"How's that?"

"I asked if you were a writer, and you said was. In other words you used to be a writer."

"I suppose."

"You say it without even thinking."

"What was," I began.

"Is," he finished.

What was is.

Or what was, stopped.

7

C hit Chat Auditorium had red seats, and plenty of windows on each side that looked out onto trees and flowers and lawns. Caron seemed big on trees and flowers and lawns. They spread out and up in every direction.

The auditorium was small, could hold maybe two hundred people, perhaps more, and this was where, a guy with buzzed brown hair told me, we spent half our lives.

He had brown eyes, was very thin, and he said, "Always wear a jacket or sweatshirt to Chit Chat. It's a fucking meat locker in there. They don't want people falling asleep during lectures and meetings."

I thought he was joking. Then I looked around and several people standing in the lobby and waiting to go inside appeared more than half asleep. A cluster of women, looking as beaten down as the men, had come in at the far side of the lobby.

They were in their late twenties to sixties, many wore sweats and Polar fleece, flip flops, and had their hair tied back or up. And if you looked close enough at some you could see scars from cutting on their legs and arms. One doe-eyed woman had scars on her neck. With nearly all of them, there was sadness in their eyes, a hauntedness.

Men sat on the right, women on the left of the aisle.

By the time I sat down I began to count, and was surprised by how many were in the auditorium. There were well over a hundred patients, and I had no idea where all of us had come from.

I asked a bald guy, two seats over, where all these people were from, and he said, "Relapse, Adolescent, Extended Care, Women's, Men's Primary. All over."

Then I saw a pink jacket, and Juliet from detox was sitting in the middle of several other women. She caught my eye, we waved, and the place seemed almost festive.

A tall handsome man with a mustache started talking. His name was Doug, and he grew up in Maine with the woods as his backyard, and now he worked here at Caron and he was going to talk about powerlessness, because he didn't think any of us knew a thing about powerlessness, No, sir. No way. Not us. We were too smart. Too special.

He paused and looked out over the rows of us.

Doug wore a tan suitcoat, jeans, a blue shirt. He had keys and a name card on his belt. There were two pens in the breast pocket of his suit coat.

He said, "I was driving up here in my car tonight. Pretty nice car. Paid for. Less than fifty thousand miles on this car, and I was listening to a cd in the stereo, a cd my son burned for me.

"And I thought, Boy, is that illegal, having a cd my son burned for me? What if the cops pulled me over for going too fast? Or using the wrong lane? And what if they saw that burned cd? Would they arrest me?"

Then he thought of the number of times he'd driven drunk.

"Anyone here ever drive drunk?"

Hands went up, slowly at first, then more and more.

Doug paused in front of a woman on the aisle who did not have her hand up. She had blond hair pulled back into a loose ponytail, and she looked sleepy.

He smiled at her.

"Never drove drunk?"

"I've never driven a car."

"Ah."

"If I did I probably would have driven drunk."

People laughed.

Doug had eventually driven with guns, big bags of pills, pounds of heroin, with things so scary and wrong that had he been stopped and searched he'd be in state prison now. Not driving up here and worrying about the CD his son burned for him.

"I have a closet at home bigger than the cell I'd be sharing," Doug said.

Our addiction, the disease of our addiction, was much much bigger than any one of us. We were powerless in the face of that addiction. That disease, unless it was treated, would kill us.

He paused for a long time. He looked up and down each row. He seemed to look for a long time in each of our eyes.

Doug had been straight and sober twenty-two years. Doug was as powerless today as he was twenty-two years ago.

He didn't know why he was standing there and we were sitting where we were.

"You know what the difference was?" he wanted to know.

Once again, he paused a long time. He looked us over. Paused more.

"Nothing," he said.

Know why?

Another pause.

"Because he was as far away from his next drink or drug as we were."

Outdoors, the sun had dipped into the woods and the light was softer. There had to be sixty or seventy people outside the Chit Chat doors, under the bell tower, standing on the road, and lighting up at the Butt Hut.

I noticed one tall guy who was several feet away from the group. He was standing very erect, and he looked ripped, looked very much like a weightlifter. He had a ponytail that reached nearly to his waist, and he kept his hands folded in front of him, beneath his belt.

He had sharp handsome features, and he looked almost familiar to me. Then I realized that I didn't know him, but that I had seen that ponytail, that weightlifter's body and that stance—in Auburn Prison.

Marcel came up to me and asked if I needed a smoke, but I said no, I had some.

He was wearing a multi-colored hoodie, zipped, and I was wearing a blue ski jacket.

"Least neither of us froze," he said, and giggled.

I lit up, blew smoke at the sky.

"Hey, professor," another guy said.

He was thirty-five maybe, muscular, had a goatee, and short hair. He was wearing Duke University sweats. Blue to match the sky. His sleeves were pushed up to his biceps, and his arms were covered with tattoos. Snakes, dragons, a sword and shield, the name Roxy.

He took out a pack of Newports. I had Kools, Marcel had Canadian menthols.

"How you doing, Jim?" I said to him, and he said, "Jim? Fucking Jim?"

"Bob?" I said. "Dave?"

"He's fucking Chuck. Tattoo Chuck."

They laughed.

I said I was sorry, and Chuck said, "Dude, you're okay. You're on drugs."

"He's on a lotta fucking drugs," Marcel said.

"Not much," I said. "Damn little."

"Look at this," Chuck said. He pulled his jacket and tee shirt up in front. His belly was covered by goose bumps, as though it was very cold. And it was seventy degrees out.

"Heroin," he said. "Two and a half weeks of withdrawal."

Marcel and Chuck laughed.

"I gotta call Sticks," Chuck said.

"Who," Marcel and I said at the same time.

Alan came over, stood next to Chuck.

"What's he telling you?" Alan said.

"Sticks," Marcel said.

"Chuck's dealer. Chuck loves him more than he loves his dog, and that's a lot," Alan said. He laughed his jackhammer laugh.

"Did I ever tell you I tried to sell the Colonel to Sticks?"

"What Sticks say?" I asked.

"He said, I don't want your dog."

Everyone laughed loud and long.

"Chuck, that's pathetic," Alan said.

"Yeah, but I needed some dope. Ya know."

The next event, an Alcoholics Anonymous speaker meeting, was in Chit Chat at eight. The crowd was even bigger than the one for the earlier lecture. The auditorium was at least half full.

It started, as with all AA meetings, with several readings. The AA Preamble, which began, "Alcoholics Anonymous is a fellowship of men and women who share their experience, strength and hope with each other that they may solve their common problem and help others to recover from alcoholism."

Next, someone read a brief section from the Big Book, the basic AA text, called "How It Works." It included the line, "Rarely have we seen a person fail who has thoroughly followed our path." Then came a reading of the Twelve Steps. The first said, "We admitted we were powerless over alcohol and that our lives had become unmanageable."

Finally came the Twelve Traditions, which addressed the organization of AA. The third tradition read, "The only requirement for membership is a desire to stop drinking." Originally, the authors had written that the only requirement was "an honest desire to stop drinking." Knowing alcoholics, and being both realistic and generous, they changed that to read "a desire to stop drinking."

Perhaps to start out, a dishonest desire, a part-honest desire, would do.

These readings, or at least some of them, were read at the beginning of virtually all AA meetings. I had been to plenty of meetings in my life, but never in rehab.

Ted was tall, and looked strong. He wore a tie that had lots of bright colors—orange, lemon, lime, raspberry. He was so bald the lights from the ceiling of Chit Chat reflected off of his head.

He spoke in a clear powerful voice.

He said he was glad to be here. Ted was lucky to be here, because by any rights he should be in state prison for armed robbery, for the distribution and sale of narcotics, for assault and battery. About a hundred counts. Five hundred counts.

"More than that," he said, and here he paused and looked up and looked us over, just the way Dave or Don or Doug—the guy earlier—had done.

"More than that," he said, and here his powerful voice got real low, and it rumbled, then got smooth.

"I should be dead."

He stepped back from the mike, from the podium, and he put his arms out at his sides.

"About a thousand times over, I should be ashes, or I should be this embalmed corpse in a casket, buried under the dirt and grass."

He paused again.

I thought, These pauses are good. These guys are good. They know how to use the pause. It gives so much more weight to the sentences, the words.

Damn, they were good. Ted and...Doug. That was it. Doug.

He used to be a normal kid, as much as any of us were normal kids. He watched "Leave It To Beaver" on television. He watched "Father Knows Best." He even read the Hardy Boys, Frank and Joe Hardy, and their dad, Fenton G. Hardy, world-famous detective. Their best friend, the portly chum, Chet Morton.

He looked us over and smiled.

"You don't know what the fuck I'm talking about, do you?"

More than half the people in the rows in front of me shook their heads.

"You're too young. You're way too young. I'm fifty-one. I'm an old bastard. That's why."

"How many of you read the Hardy Boys?"

I threw my hand up with about ten other people.

"God," he said.

Then he got to be thirteen, fourteen, and he drank, smoked dope, and nothing was ever the same again. He had been an athlete, a football and baseball player, a good student, even an altar boy.

Then everything went. Everything.

He got his first motorcycle by sixteen, became a felon around the same time, and that was thirty-five years ago.

He talked about guns, crack, meth, cocaine, booze, fights with pipes and chains, motorcycle gangs. He talked about stitches, broken bones, a ruptured spleen, intensive care.

Then he talked about AA, the gift of desperation, of not wanting to die. Of going to meetings, hanging out with people who were in the same leaky lifeboat he was in.

He got a sponsor in the program, a man older than him who listened, was patient beyond belief, who stayed with him year after year after year.

Then Ted paused again. "We ate dinner together. We talked every day. He even took me fishing. Imagine. Fishing."

Ted was smiling. Ted was remembering.

"Then he got cancer, bad cancer. And I was with him the whole time, and he was amazing. It was like he was showing me how to die. He never complained, never showed how much pain he was in."

He paused, and you could hear people sniffling. You could see tissues pressed to some people's eyes.

"And I thought, this is what it comes down to. How do you want to die?"

He paused. He looked at us a long time.

"In chaos and insanity?

"Or with everything in order? With peace and serenity?"

He paused again.

His eyes seemed to glow.

"How do you want to die?"

At the Butt Hut, the sky was turning a much deeper blue, almost black, and a pale piece of moon was stuck in the sky in the east. People were unusually subdued, taking out cigarettes, lighting them, handing them around.

I saw Max for the first time since the afternoon. He looked at me, then he looked away as though he'd never seen me before. He wasn't smoking, just standing by himself.

I took the patient schedule from my pocket, unfolded it, saw that the next thing was Meditation at nine-thirty. There was a small, older guy with horn-rimmed glasses standing near me. I asked him what Meditation was, and he said it was every night, was upstairs from the lounge, down the hall in what they called the meat locker.

Another meat locker, I thought.

"It's pretty fast," he said. "Usually twenty minutes."

I walked up the road, past the giant pine trees and the long bed of flowers to the small gazebo. The woods were getting darker and darker, and I couldn't see any squirrels or birds.

At the crest of the hill I kept walking, down, down, past the beautiful stone building, till I could just make out dark hills and valleys way off. Then I came to the top of some wide stairs, and at the bottom was a building with double doors and a wood cutout of a chef.

The cafeteria.

Ah. Pretty shrewd, I thought. I'm a sleuth.

Almost time for meditation.

Most people were gone from the Butt Hut. Now, it seemed, in an instant, the twilight was gone, and shadows from lights were long. I'd begun to feel weird and nervous again, as though bad things, things I couldn't name, were going to happen.

The darkness seemed full of whispers and shadows.

There were footsteps behind me.

I looked back. A man was walking quickly toward me.

I saw keys on his belt. I saw his I.D. badge.

He said hello. He moved past fast.

He had the same walk as my father's, a quick, nervous walk. My father had been a hard-working man—two jobs for much of my childhood. He had never smoked cigarettes, never drank, never even had coffee or tea; he used to plead with me to stop smoking. He was so quietly pleased when I did well in college, and when I got into graduate school, he took a thousand-dollar loan out for me so that I could put a down payment on an apartment in Ithaca, and buy books.

There was a breeze now and the top branches of trees were swaying in the air.

Meditation was in the Meat Locker, up a stairway from the lounge, then down a hallway, past ten or twelve staff offices, all of which were closed. It was the size of a small classroom, only it was windowless, featureless, and had chairs. There was a table near the door, and Levon sat on it next to a boom box.

About a dozen chairs were grouped in an oval.

I sat down with seven or eight guys, and a C.A., a woman in her forties who wore glasses and shoes with silver buckles on top. She didn't look at me, but most of the other guys said, Hello, and Welcome, and, Hey.

"Okay," Bert said. "Here we go." He looked around. "All set?"

"Let's get it done," Alan said.

A man who looked like an Aztec warrior, with heavy black glasses, began to read from a small book.

"Just for today I might try out a new attitude as often as possible, in as many situations as possible," he began.

A new attitude was like looking through new windows or trying on new glasses, he continued. It offered the chance of seeing the world anew, of new possibilities in life. It meant not trying to change the world, which was a very tall order, some might say an impossible order, but trying to change ourselves, or at least our attitude, and that was very much within our reach.

"Thursday, May 21," he said.

He closed the book, then he said, "Rafael, addict."

Everyone said, "Rafael."

He said today had been a pretty good day. He talked to his mother, and that went well. Went to the gym and that was always good. Welcome to Paul. Good to have you here. With that I pass.

"Support you, Rafe," the guys said.

The next guy was Toby, who was in his sixties. He was short, and powerfully built, and had a deep raspy voice.

He'd had a good day too. He met with his counselor, and thought the speakers were good. And he said it was especially good to have someone from upstate New York here. So, nice to have you, professor.

By the time it reached me, all but one person had welcomed me, and I wasn't sure what to say.

I started to talk without saying my name.

People said, "Who are you?

"I'm Paul and I'm an addict."

I thanked everyone for making me feel so welcome. I still felt pretty clueless about everything, and my brain was gonna take a while to come back. But thanks again. And yeah, the speakers were terrific, especially the Theo guy. How do you want to die?

Several people started laughing.

"Ted."

"Yeah, Ted."

A few more people went. Then someone read from a sheet.

"Were we kind, compassionate, thoughtful today?" it began. "Did we treat everyone we encountered with patience and love? When we were wrong did we promptly admit it?"

Then there was a reading of the Prayer of Saint Francis. "Lord, make me an instrument of Thy peace. Where there is hatred, let me sow love." All the way to, "For it is in dying that we are born to eternal life."

Levon shut the lights off, and the room was utterly dark. He hit a button, and the room was flooded with bird sounds, harp and flute music. It sifted and flowed and filtered over us, and for three or four minutes we sat silently.

I felt my breath under the music, felt my hands on the armrests of the chair, my feet on the carpet, and thought, I really am here. I'm here.

He shut the music off, turned the lights on, and Alan said, "Bring it in, boys."

Everyone got in the middle of the room in a circle and put their arms around each other.

A sleepy guy name Arnold with a black and gray goatee said, "Left foot back for all the shit we leave on the mountain," and everyone moved their left foot back a step.

"Right foot forward for all the good things to come." Right feet went forward. "Heads held high, they've been down too long." People lifted their heads.

"Oh my…"

"God," everyone said, "grant me the serenity to accept the things I cannot change, the courage to change the things I can, and the wisdom to knoooooowwww the difference." Guys held the word *know* for at least ten seconds.

Back in the lounge I remembered that I got a bedtime detox med. I thought that this would be my last time getting Ativan four times a day. Tomorrow I went down to three times a day.

Funny how I could remember the detox protocol, the drugs, with such precision.

I was going through the kitchen gallery when Bert asked me if I was going to burn one. Detox med, I said, then I'll burn one.

Outside it was windy, and the trees and bushes made long, weird shadows from the security lights. I walked between light and shadow, found my way to the detox, through the halls, to my lone pill.

On the way back the wind had picked up, and I thought of nights a long time ago, in junior high school, in winter, standing outside a liquor store in Newton, with my friends Bob and Lee, asking people going in if they would buy for us. Always, someone would.

A six-pack of beer, a bottle of wine, a half-pint of vodka and rum. We'd break the six-pack up, stuff cans into our pockets, mix the vodka with orange juice, the rum with coke. And we'd walk and sip, sip and walk, would feel the warmth spread.

No matter how cold it was, if it was ten or twenty degrees out, we didn't care because within a half hour or hour we were pretty drunk. We'd tell stories and jokes, and laugh and stare at the starlit sky. That numb, sweet feeling filled us. Being young and drunk, warm in the cold. We were never going to feel pain.

I heard laughter up the road. It was the guys at the Butt Hut. The guys in rehab.

The guys like me.

8

T hirty guys crowded into the lounge, and every one of them seemed to be yelling at once. Yelling, Fuck you, Hey, Dude, Man, yelling, Holy shit. The words crank, vodka, smashed, fucked-up, blitzed, vikes, percs, Jack, and junk were thrown around the way handicaps were tossed around a country club locker room.

"You're in rehab, dude," someone said, and I saw Max talking to Toby, the older guy with the gravel voice. Max was a foot taller than him, but could not have weighed as much. Max was still wearing the worn suitjacket, and I could see threads dangling from the elbows, lapels and pockets like tinsel from a Christmas tree.

Bert asked me if I wanted to burn one, and I told him I'd pass. For now.

In one of the big blue chairs Arnold was sleeping, actually sleeping. His mouth was open.

Chuck was laughing loud at something Rafael was saying. It seemed warm in the lounge, but Chuck had a parka and watch cap on over his Duke sweats. I remembered the goose bumps on his stomach. I thought of Sticks, his dealer. I wondered where Colonel, his dog, was.

I was leaning against a cabinet next to the fireplace. The room seemed to jump and bounce and buzz. Everyone moved constantly, made noise. It was monkeys in a cage. You heard again and again that addiction to alcohol or drugs was a disease of isolation. That it cut you off from family, friends, work, finally from love. There wasn't room for anything else.

Maybe that was one of the strategies of Caron. Throw us in together. Anti-isolation.

Max sidled up, and asked me if I wanted to take a walk. He twitched and blinked.

I told him I was meeting Bert for a smoke.

Levon said he'd come.

We pushed past a compact guy my age in the kitchen. He wore tiny rimless glasses and looked fit.

"Hey, Doc," Levon said.

In a deep voice Doc said, "Levon."

"Doc, this is Professor Paul."

"Yes, we met," Doc said.

I had no memory of meeting him.

"Hope you sleep tonight," he said. "Benzodiazepines murder sleep."

He knew I did benzos. He knew the full name of benzos. How'd he know?

We pushed outside, and the night had turned cool. I had to remember that we were on, if not a mountain, then a fairly serious hill. The weather seemed to change hour by hour. The temperature had dropped by twenty-five degrees since dinnertime, from seventy to forty-five. With the wind it seemed more like thirty-five.

"What kind of doc is Doc?" I asked Levon.

We were coming close to the Butt Hut, and in the dark I could make out five or six guys. Their smokes glowed orange in the dark.

"Doc Devin's a hematologist."

"Why's he here?

"Ambien. Doc was taking twenty, thirty a day."

He told me that Doc and Arnold, the sleeping guy, were on the two biggest detox loads he knew of. They started at twenty-four milligrams of Ativan a day. Arnold slept all the time, Doc lay awake in bed nearly the whole night.

Arnold was so snowed that when he walked down a hall he'd bump the wall on one side, then the other side, back to the other side. Until he'd hit the wall, not bounce, stay on the wall, and fall asleep, eventually sliding to the floor. People had to wake him at the end of every lecture, meditation and meeting.

I asked what Arnold had used, and Levon said Ambien and pain pills.

"A lot?" I asked.

"A ton, for something like ten or fifteen years."

And Arnold must have been a pretty sharp guy, he said, underneath all the sleep, because he had owned some kind of printing business in New York City that he sold for fifteen, twenty million dollars.

"Arnold?" I said.

"Arnold.'

That was the thing about people in here, he said. It was amazing how bright and successful they were. But you only saw that after the first weeks when the drugs were getting out of their bodies. It was like seeing the dead awake.

Tim, the silent Vietnam guy, was at the Butt Hut, handsome Ricky, Bert, big Jake, and three other guys I didn't know. All of them were smoking except for Jake, and Jake was chewing tobacco and spitting. It looked like a late-night bus station, everyone waiting for a ride to somewhere.

More and more, there was a feeling of being cut off from the larger world. There were no calendars, very limited access to computers or phones, no regular books or magazines, no television or radio, no stereos or CD players. We could read recovery literature, and we could talk to the staff and to each other.

An airplane went by high overhead, going east to west, probably from Philadelphia which was about an hour to the east. It was a line of blinking lights in the sky, red, blue, white. I pictured the interior of the cabin, the passengers settling down for a long flight, with blankets, neck pillows, books and magazines, laptops. Going somewhere.

I thought of Dallas, St. Louis, Chicago, Denver, Las Vegas, Los Angeles, San Francisco, Seattle, Vancouver. Vancouver was a nice city.

"How the fuck you doing, professor?" Bert asked.

"Good."

"They showing you around okay?"

"Yep."

"Bert," Levon said.

"Junkie."

"Thank you," Levon said. "I like when you call me Junkie."

"You're welcome." Bert nodded. He puffed on his Marlboro. He lifted his head, sniffed the dark air. His big white mustache seemed almost electric, seemed to glow.

It was 10:25 on the bell tower clock. The schedule listed eleven as bedtime, and Marcel had said that the outside doors were locked at eleven. If you wanted to have a smoke between eleven and six you told the overnight C.A., and you went outside.

Wake-up was 6:30, so that only left time for seven and a half hours sleep.

I heard the snap of a lighter, saw the brief small flame, beyond the Adirondack chairs, near the trees and the edge of the little cliff. There was a guy standing, facing the dark woods. He was long and thin, seemed to be wearing a vest over the untucked tails of a shirt.

He turned, took a pull on his smoke, and it was something like seeing a ghost, like somebody from an earlier life.

It was Gavin—the name that meant white hawk in Welsh—from the detox lounge. I was surprised I could remember him. The smile was gone.

I walked across the gravel, threaded my way through the chairs, and said, "Gavin."

He almost jumped, turned fast.

He looked at me, arms raised in something like a shaky fighting posture, and said, "Who the fuck are you?"

"Paul, from detox."

I smiled, offered my hand.

He didn't see my hand, or ignored it.

"I don't know you, dude." He looked at me with no trace of smile. "But lemme tell you something."

I watched his tight, unsmiling face.

"Don't ever creep up on me again. Never. Not ever."

He looked at me.

I was going to look away, but didn't think I should.

"You try it again, you get hurt."

He looked at me some more. He was sixty years old. He couldn't have weighed a hundred and fifty pounds and he was shaking badly.

"I'm sorry," I said.

He didn't seem to hear me.

"You understand?"

He turned and looked into the woods.

I stood and wasn't sure what to say or do.

"Motherfucker's in withdrawal," Bert said.

I felt a thick heavy arm on my shoulders, and Jake said, "Professor, people can be pretty paranoid sometimes."

Everyone at the Butt Hut had heard me and Gavin.

"He was such a nice guy in detox," I said.

Levon threw his butt on the ground, scattering sparks like fireworks. "Wait an hour," he said. "You'll get a different guy."

A tall, bald guy, maybe my age, said, "Fuck him. He's just a dick." His name was Kipp and he was a lawyer in Relapse.

Kipp said he didn't give a shit what the guy was going through. There was no excuse. We all hated this place. We all couldn't wait to leave.

I looked around at the lights from the low building, at the trees and bushes and flowers, at the dark sky. My cigarette tasted awful, and I couldn't imagine wanting another one for a long time.

A door farther up the building opened and closed, and a big guy, not huge like Jake, but big, came out. He had a deep voice, like a classical actor.

He said, "Hey professor."

His name was Hal, and he had a shy smile. He was a drunk, he said, with pills thrown in, and he was also a high school English teacher.

"I hear we got that in common," he said.

We do, I said, then asked him what kind of pills he did.

Pain pills, Valium and clonazepam.

I said, "Same here. Bingo."

He said he knew. He'd heard.

I could see the teacher in him, the inclined head, the concern on his face.

He had very fair skin, with childhood freckles, visible even in the dark.

I asked how long he'd been here and he said seventeen days. He said he was a high-bottom drunk and addict, like me. Good job, money, no jail or gutters. But it was pretty bad.

He looked at me, and there was something in his look that was very much like his voice—it went deep down.

He was dying, he said. He was really on his way out, and he was dying ugly.

He paused, pursed his lips.

So coming here, well, it wasn't easy, it wasn't fun, but it wasn't supposed to be. This was tough and rigorous, but we were dealing with matters of life and death. This disease wanted to kill us.

"More and more," he said, "Caron's the place of not dying. This is a place of life."

Then Hal was quiet and I was quiet, and after a few minutes I realized there were no other voices. Gavin was gone.

I looked around and everyone had gone, had disappeared inside.

The belltower clock read ten-fifty.

Hal said he best go in, and he moved quietly away.

I lit one more cigarette, and smoked it quickly down. The place felt funny with nobody there. Just wind and shadows. Things you could see or feel but couldn't touch.

Light was that way too, I thought. It existed. You could see it, and it made the difference between day and night.

But you couldn't touch light, couldn't box it or bottle it. Light wasn't something you could hold in your hands.

Inside, there were less than half the number of guys in the lounge as there had been, and it was way more quiet. I got juice from the big silver juice machine in the kitchen, was standing and drinking and watching, when Dave, the C.A., came out and said, "Okay, guys."

He closed the curtains on the windows on the far side of the lounge, dimmed the lights, and a guy I'd never seen before started straightening books and newspapers on the coffee table.

"Hey thanks, Matt," Dave said, and I wondered where Matt had been all day and night.

Levon and Doc and Chuck and Marcel were still sitting around. So was a dark-haired guy I thought I'd seen but couldn't name.

Levon said, "You gonna try to sleep?"

"Why the fuck bother?" Chuck said.

"You guys still not sleeping?" Dave asked.

Chuck looked at him with disgust, Levon said, "Got some Ambien?" and Doc said, "Where have you been?"

"Off," Dave said. "Hey, I got a life. May not seem that way but I do."

"Getting an hour a night," Chuck said.

"Two here," Levon said.

"Better not get more than that, motherfucker. Don't leave me," Chuck said.

He and Levon laughed. They put their arms around each other for a moment. Two heroin guys, both alike in dignity, in Caron where we lay our scene.

After a few minutes, I said goodnight, and went to my bedroom. I put on sweatpants, brushed my teeth, pulled down the covers of my bed, opened the windows next to the bed, shut the light off. Cool air blew in.

I got in bed, stretched down under the covers, and almost began to laugh. My feet were hanging a foot over the end.

I lay like a corpse, arms at my sides, hands folded on my stomach, legs together, head straight. My feet were still way the hell over the edge and uncovered. I could feel the night air on them.

I opened my eyes and looked up. There was pale ceiling. Only that.

I turned over, facing the window. The air was so cool it was almost cold. Maybe it was cold; it was forty fucking degrees out. I didn't know, couldn't tell. I was feeling the withdrawal flow in like a tide. I wasn't sure of much of anything. I was a middle-aged guy lying alone in the dark.

Shit. This sucked. This shaking. This weird feeling.

I was gonna jump and scream. I was gonna bang my head against a wall.

Breathe, I said. Breathe slow, breathe deep.

In, one two three four.

Out, one two three four.

I did that for two or three minutes.

Maybe it was a minute. I didn't know, couldn't tell.

Nothing was sure. Nothing.

Fuck. Fuck.

God, grant me the serenity.

Hail Mary, full of grace.

I couldn't remember anything after that.

Two years with the nuns, first and second grade of Parochial school, a good Irish-Catholic boy, and I couldn't remember the basic prayer.

Fucking sinner.

Oh my God I am heartily sorry for having offended Thee.

And that was it.

Our Father Who Art in heaven, hallowed be Thy name.

Again, a stone wall.

The Hail Mary, The Act of Contrition, The Our Father. The big three. I used to know them like breathing.

Then I remembered a woman at an AA meeting way back who talked about a prayer she said, because she barely believed in a God, didn't know what God was. But she said it because it was short, impossible to forget, and easy. She could say it fifty times in the checkout line at the grocery store.

God help. God help. God help, she said.

I started to say it, lying in bed.

God help, God help, God help, God help.

I said it again and again.

Then it struck me that it was two syllables, ba bump, ba bump, like a heartbeat.

So I lay there in the dark for I don't know how long.

I said it to myself.

God help. God help.

Ba bump, ba bump, my heart sounded.

God help.

Ba bump.

9

T he night was silent as six feet under. No blip or beep. No sound anywhere.

I pushed a button on my watch and the ghostly green light came on. Eleven-thirty-seven.

Eleven-thirty-seven! I hadn't even been in bed an hour. It felt like three nights already.

In detox I slept so much that days and nights swam. Saturday was Monday, Monday was Wednesday.

Now the seconds crept along breath by breath.

I didn't feel too weird at the moment, just restless and a little trapped. I got up to use the bathroom. When the bathroom door snapped shut it went "Bang" like a gunshot.

I jumped.

When I flushed the toilet it went "Boom" like a bomb.

I nearly hit the deck.

Then I stood in front of the mirror in the bright light, and watched myself. It was me but not me. My hair was dark and very long. It hung down on each side of my face, and I peered out as though through the bars of a cage.

How long since I'd had a haircut?

If I stopped shaving I'd look like a man who lived in a shack in the woods. Ate meals out of cans. Scared people.

I sat on the side of my bed, and tried to breathe slowly, but I couldn't bring myself to do it.

Then I got up, went out to the hall, and was startled.

It wasn't the same place as it was in the day. The lights were dim, and it was absolutely empty and utterly quiet. Colors were muted, shapes were shadowed.

I looked to the right, down the long hall toward Chit Chat. It had to have been sixty or seventy feet long, and there were only closed doors and a solitary red EXIT sign at the far end.

The lounge was very dark. I went in, sat down in a blue chair, and saw a dark figure lying on the couch near the far wall. I couldn't tell who it was, just that he seemed to have a watch cap pulled down over his face, and he seemed to be sleeping.

I sat for five minutes, ten minutes, and it didn't seem so bad, sitting in the lounge rather than lying in bed.

"Professor," I heard.

I looked from my hands to the sleeping form, back to my hands.

"Levon," I said.

"Chuck. Welcome to the night."

I laughed.

"Can't sleep?"

"Oh, no," I said.

He sat up. He was wearing a parka and a watch cap pulled low on his forehead.

"How long since you've slept?" I asked.

"Fuck if I know."

We were silent. We listened to quiet.

"I slept a few nights in detox. Since then I get an hour or two a night."

"Can't they give you anything?"

We looked at each other, then we both began to laugh.

"Forget it," I said. "I never said that."

"An aspirin. They give you an aspirin. Motherfuckers."

We laughed some more.

Chuck was from New York City, on his seventeenth day in rehab. He was thirty-one, and he'd been an addict, more on than off, since his late teens. He had worked as a personal trainer before he was too fucked-up to work anymore.

Plus his cell phone, he added. That's how he got in touch with Sticks.

"You wanna go for a smoke?"

I said, Sure.

He said I better get a coat. It always got cold out. And if you were withdrawing it was the Arctic.

Last night he saw snow and sleet out there. "Swear to God," he said. "Fucking snow and sleet in May."

We laughed some more.

I couldn't tell exactly how cold it was at the Butt Hut, just that it seemed like February in Ithaca.

Chuck gave me a Newport, I gave him a Kool, and with the wind it took us about four flicks of the lighter to get them lit.

Chuck told me about Riker's Island, where he spent a year. Narcotics possession, second arrest.

It was a city, he said. Huge. So many buildings. Made Caron look tiny.

Not so many flowers and trees either.

Lots of weights. Chuck said he got really big. Ate right, slept, got pretty fucking healthy. At fucking Riker's. Feature that.

The problem was, he said, that he had an earlier dealer who dealt out of an apartment. All's the cops had to do was park across the street, and pop anyone who walked out.

Sticks was smart. Sticks didn't have an apartment where he sold dope.

He was real tall and real skinny. All bones and tendons.

He wore these tiny little glasses that were tinted red, and the lenses, he swore, were the size of quarters. And Sticks had short spiked hair, and he had a pit bull named Albus. Shit you not, Chuck said, after the guy in Harry Potter.

I sat back, pulled on a Kool, and felt the wind blow, and looked at shadows.

Chuck sat back in his chair, and said that it was good to have someone to talk to at this hour.

"I can't tell you how many hours I've sat here by myself. Then me and Levon, thank God. Couple of dope fiends."

He said he wouldn't mind being alone at all if he was shooting dope. Like who gave a shit when you were high.

"Know what I mean?" he said.

I nodded, then I thought he might not be able to see me in the dark.

"Exactly," I said. "You're in your own little world."

"They could fucking kill you and you wouldn't notice."

The thing Sticks did that his other dealer would never think to do was use cars.

"Cars?" I said.

Cars, Chuck said. Three of them. A Ford, a Chevy, and a Honda. None of them new, one blue, one green, one gray.

He'd use one for a week, then switch, use that one for a week, then switch to a third car. And he was always moving around, one street to another, one neighborhood to another neighborhood. All over Queens. Never knew where he'd be.

"I had to call him for a location, and sometimes I'd get there, and I'd have to call for another location, and once in awhile I'd get to the second location and I'd have to call for a third place.

"If I couldn't find the motherfucker, the cops couldn't find the motherfucker either."

"Did Sticks ever get busted?"

"Nope."

I smiled at Chuck.

"Nope rhymes with dope."

We giggled like grade school kids.

"How's that, professor? Nope and dope."

"Say nope to dope."

"Think we could make money on that?" Chuck asked.

"Big money. Big big money. Kick Nancy Reagan's ass."

"Just say no kind of sucked."

"Really sucked."

We sat quietly like deep thinkers. Two men with killer insight.

There was a low light showing on the bell tower clock. Twelve-thirty-two.

It was cold.

"Where's your winter coat?" Chuck said.

"It's back in January. God. It's late May."

"Dude," he said, "we're on a fucking mountain in Pennsylvania. We got bears and wolverines up here. We got Yeti and Bigfoot. We got snow and sleet all summer. Welcome to the country. Welcome to Pennsylvania. Know what I'm saying?"

My teeth started to chatter. I could feel goosebumps on my arms.

Chuck had pulled his hood up over his watch cap. He looked like Alaska. Like frozen tundra and dog sleds and igloos. Not some guy from Queens kicking heroin in a rehab. He looked kind of wholesome.

I started to shake all over.

"You wanna borrow my coat?" Chuck said.

"Thanks. Couldn't do it. Couldn't watch you shiver."

So we went in.

It seemed even darker and quieter than before. It felt like I could feel all those guys breathing deep and regular and sleeping. I wondered how many of them were dreaming about booze and drugs—beer and vodka, gin and wine, whiskey, rum, brandy, bourbon, benzos, Percocet, vikes, coke, meth, inhalants, codeine, methadone, heroin, Fentanyl. God, there were so many. In here I heard of things I'd never heard of. And I'd been here? I wasn't sure how long. Five days, seven days.

It seemed forever.

It seemed no time.

I went into my room, closed the window, and got in bed. Under the covers, I started to get toasty.

My watch said one-twenty-eight. With a six-thirty wake-up I could get five hours sleep. It seemed like everyone in here slept well. Or almost everyone. Not Chuck or Levon or Doc.

When my sons were very small they were terrible sleepers, both of them. From the time he got home from the hospital, it seemed, Liam cried so often during the night that neither of us got much more than an hour or two of consecutive sleep, for five or six months. We walked around punchy and stupid, in gray days and blue nights.

We thought it was for the rest of our life, and started to gets colds all the time, and became clumsy cooks and poor drivers.

Somewhere in his sixth month, for reasons we did not understand, Liam began to sleep through the night. That awful, throaty, cacophony of sound that was his cry, the sound that still terrifies me, was gone.

I closed my eyes, breathed slow and deep.

Then I thought of something amazing. Something I was pretty sure was not a fantasy or dream.

At home, in my office, when Liz and I cleaned out the drugs, I didn't tell her about one last stash.

In the second row of books, in the far right corner, there were about sixty-five codeine tablets in a plastic bag.

That wasn't an especially large amount, nor was codeine all that powerful. But it was a narcotic, and that would last me a week. Well, four or five days.

But it would be just enough to help me settle back in after returning from Caron, before I got serious about recovery. It would give me a little cushion.

You fucking addict, I thought. What a moron.

But it wasn't my fault. I didn't even remember about the stash till now. I didn't plan it or anything.

Did I?

Here I was, dropping almost thirty grand on rehab, and I had a plan to get wasted the minute I got out.

For God's sake. Sixty-five codeine was not that many and they weren't that strong. And they were codeine-three, which was kind of medium strength.

How was it I could remember this, the number of pills, the strength, with such precision, and I could barely remember the names of people?

Fucking druggie.

I breathed some more, and felt kind of warm. The pills were in a sealed plastic bag. They were flat, white, and had a large number three etched in one side of them. For the first time in days I felt something like hope, as though an old girlfriend had called.

Seven minutes of two.

Tomorrow was going to be a gray day.

But I felt more relaxed than I had since I'd been here.

I could feel it in my feet, legs, torso, chest, now even in my head. The slow and sleepy feeling.

I counted backwards. One hundred, ninety-nine, ninety-eight, ninety-seven, ninety-six.

I blinked awake, and didn't know where I was. I never knew where I was for the first seconds after waking. There was different furniture, odd dimensions. The wall beyond my feet was much closer than at home. There were no bookcases. My wife was not sleeping beside me. And I felt raw yet foggy, as though I had not slept at all.

Auuuggghhh.

Rehab. The same fucking place. Caron Treatment Center for nine hundred bucks a day. Still in the same skin. Still Paul Cody, addict.

My watch said four-seventeen. So I had probably slept two hours, or not quite. Maybe an hour-forty-five.

Dr. Troncale had told me that at some point I'd probably experience significant sleep disturbance.

"Significant sleep disturbance." Such a delicate phrase. There was nothing of the thrashing, the tossing, the relentless thoughts.

At two-sixteen, two-seventeen, two-twenty, two-twenty-one. At four-thirty-three and four-thirty-six.

Two hours sleep made for a very protracted and grim day. A day that was twenty-two hours long, and where everything seemed distant and slightly unreal.

I got up to use the bathroom, trying to keep the door from popping like a gunshot, but it fired anyway.

Four fucking a.m. and the bastards at Caron were firing guns with their doors, to wake us up, shake us up, snap us out of it. Out of the drug and booze-addled vapor. Same with the toilets. Bombs. Fucking bombs at four a.m.

God help, I said. I said it five or ten times.

My hands and arms were moving. They wouldn't be still. They rattled, danced, throbbed. My shoulders jumped every five seconds or so.

In the bathroom mirror I didn't look so weird. Just the jungle hair, and the start of a beard.

Fuck fuck fuck.

I went out to the lounge, and someone in the dark said, "Dude."

I saw a lump under blankets, a cushion over its face.

He lifted the cushion.

Levon.

"You sleep?" I asked.

"Little."

"Where's Chuck?"

"He went to try to sleep, maybe twenty minutes ago."

He got up, came over and sat on the couch next to me. It felt amazing and wonderful to have him there. A warm body, a human being. Not my overheated, fevered brain.

"You get any sleep?" he said.

"I think."

"You think."

Even though he was bald and his ears kind of stuck out, and he had tattoos all over the place, including his neck and skull, Levon looked almost normal in the dark. His eyes were large, seemed alert, and had nothing of sleep in them.

"You wanna smoke?" he said.

I said I would, just that I was freezing earlier when I was out with Chuck.

I was still rattling, still moving and jumping when I didn't mean to.

Levon got up, said, "Be right back."

Then I remembered the pills, the codeine in my office. I felt almost exposed, thinking about it out here in the lounge. As though people could see into my brain, or catch the druggie brain waves.

I could picture being up in my office alone. Finding the baggie, taking out the pills. Then one, then two, then three.

How quiet they would make me. How numb and simple and silent. It wouldn't take long. Twenty minutes.

The shakes were gone. Like a contact hit. I held my hand out in front of me. God. Holy cow. Pills. Three weeks away.

Levon came back and threw a coat to me. He said his dad brought him a coat, then his brother brought him a coat.

"It's fucking freezing," Levon said.

I stood up, tried the coat on, laughed. It was pretty long, but not wide. I could get my arms in the sleeves, and zip the front, but it was tight as sausage casing.

The wind was even more intense than before. The leaves and branches were thrashing. They were tossing, like they meant to jump from their trunks.

I warmed up inside the coat fast. When I asked Levon, he said it was down. I asked what a kid in New York City was doing with a down coat, and he said every kid on the Upper West Side had a down coat.

"Chuck?" I asked.

Chuck was from Queens. Chuck's coat was Quallofil, one of those synthetic insulations. Chuck's neighborhood was small single houses with little yards with chain-link fences. Chuck's dad worked for the Transit Authority, probably made a bundle, great union. Levon lived in a building with a doorman, a view of the park. His dad worked on Wall Street, Mom was a lawyer.

"Big fucking difference, down and Quallofil," Levon said.

We lit cigarettes, and I smoked mine without taking my hands from my pockets. With my hands in my pockets and the hood up, I felt like I was under the covers in bed.

Then I wondered if Chuck's coat had been this warm.

He offered his parka to me.

I looked over and Levon was staring into the dark, thrashing trees. I wondered what he saw.

Then I thought that in the last few hours, two heroin addicts, two junkies from New York City, had offered me their coats. And here I was with one of the junkies, in his coat, on a mountaintop in rural Pennsylvania.

I was an addict too, and I was quite warm.

10

November, and I was forty-eight years old. It was about ten on a Friday night, and I was tired, standing in our kitchen, our clean, well-lit kitchen with the dark red counters, the black and white tiled floor.

Everything was neat, picked-up, squared away.

I had taught several seminars that day, then done office hours. And the students had lined up to see me. For three hours they came in, to talk about their papers, to talk about their parents who were getting divorced, to talk about their drinking, about their cutting.

One thin young woman rolled up the sleeve of her blouse and showed me the bright red cuts that ran up and down her forearms. The cuts were not deep but they were close to a foot long, on both the inside and outside parts of her arm.

"How often do you cut?" I asked.

She cried and said, "More and more."

I got her to call the health center from my office and make an appointment with a therapist.

This kind of thing happened, these bleeding, broken kids seemed to show up in my office all the time. When you taught Personal Essay, this delving into personal pain occurred, and spilled from the classroom into my office.

That was one of the most surprising things about so many of the college students I taught. They seemed so bright, strong, healthy and confident. And of course so many were.

But so many were not. Or they were and they weren't.

So standing in the kitchen, it had been a long day.

First teaching, then talking with students, then home for dinner, cleaning up, baths for the kids, reading to kids, bedtime for kids. Liam and Austin were nine and six. Liz worked half-time.

With the lights in the kitchen on, all I could see in the window behind the sink was my own reflection. I turned them off, and suddenly, in the dark kitchen, I could see the big side yard, then our neighbors' house, a handsome Federal that was more than a hundred and fifty years old.

It occurred to me that I was almost fifty years old, and that I was a college professor. Our house was paid off, we had enough money, a solid marriage, healthy, bright kids, lots of friends, published books, good jobs. Then I thought, not for the first time, that I had everything I had ever dreamed of having.

And I thought that I had not had a drink or used drugs in twenty-five years, to the month. A quarter of a century. That was almost a whole life.

I was a new person. A strong, confident adult, not that messed-up kid of twenty-three. I was a parent, a husband, a professor.

It would be different if I tried to drink now, a quarter century later.

The house was dark. I walked slowly through it. Dining room, hallway, living room, back through the kitchen, the room in back with all the windows that looked out onto the backyard. The trees, rooftops, the hill where I saw the lights of houses, and beyond that, Cornell.

I had a graduate degree from an Ivy League institution, for God's sake.

I went into the kitchen, turned a light on, looked in a corner cabinet. There was a bottle of bourbon that we kept for my mother-in-law when she visited. Every evening at five, before dinner, she'd have about two tablespoons of bourbon with ice and soda, and nurse it for an hour.

I found a tumbler, put in four ice cubes, and poured about six, eight ounces of bourbon. Then I spilled in maybe an ounce or two of water.

It smelled like something for removing rust, like diesel fuel, like medicine for cleaning wounds. I shut the lights off and sat in the back room. There was some moonlight, and some spidery shadows on the floor and wall from the moon and bare branches of trees.

The window was cool to the touch. I guessed it was forty degrees out, there in mid-November, with maybe ten days to go until Thanksgiving. I sat in an upholstered chair, the drink on a small table next to me.

I looked, saw the shiny cubes in the surface of the glass. Then I picked it up, sniffed, and thought, A quarter century.

Then I sipped, swallowed, coughed a little, felt the fire in my mouth, throat, belly.

And it was amazing because no matter how long it had been, a month or a year, a decade, twenty-five years—it was like no time either. It tasted the same, felt the same.

That warmth spreading through me.

I waited a minute, sipped a little more. Felt more heat inside.

It was in my blood. It was in my brain already. That fuzzy, relaxed feeling. The melting away of worry, fear, loneliness, tiredness. The world was warm. It was good and sweet, generous and kind.

No drink, not a drop in twenty-five years, and here I was having one, and this was supposed to be a disaster.

I took another sip, another sip.

Boy, was I fuzzy, and boy was I warm. I wanted to call people and tell them I loved them. I was a fucking Hallmark card. I was thinking of my mother, my two brothers and two sisters, and I was thinking of how much I loved them.

I could call my brother Shawn, tell him I loved him, and he'd probably say, "What're you, lonely?" Shawn worked sixty hours a week.

Liz was asleep, but I told her I loved her regularly anyway. Same with my boys. None of them had ever seen me drunk or high.

I'd had maybe half the drink, and I felt good. I was happy. Nothing bad had happened. Goes to show.

I started to think of the bad things I had not done. I had not burned down the house. I had not screamed at the kids, abused Liz, nor kicked the cats. I did not take the car out and drive it into a tree or telephone pole. I didn't go out into the street and howl at the moon, or curse the neighbors. I didn't kick the TV in, drink Drano, or max out the credit cards. I didn't go to casinos or visit porn chat rooms on the net.

I was a normal person, a professor, having a drink.

The glass was two thirds empty, in less than a half hour. I stood up to stretch, nearly stumbled over, grinned at myself. I thought, Man, I'm pretty drunk. This is strong shit. I won't be driving under the influence of this stuff.

And that made me think I was pretty responsible, reasonable, smart about the booze. That I would think to not drive under its influence.

I was different. Of course I wasn't the same person I was at eighteen or twenty or twenty-three. I had kids now. I had published four novels.

I sat down and finished the drink in one pull. It tasted a little watery now, compared to the first sips.

For five or ten minutes I sat and thought about all kinds of things. About how lucky I was. To be in such good health. Aside from depression, I had just about perfect health. To have enough money. To be married to Liz.

And here I was in a cushy chair, in a house we owned, that we had paid off years early because we were such good and responsible people, and I had a wicked buzz on. I was glowing like fucking candles on Christmas Eve; I had grown up, passed the danger zone, and I wasn't even an alcoholic or drug addict any more.

I'll drink to that, I thought.

So I stood up, walked unsteadily to the kitchen, brushing walls with my shoulders, leaned on the counter in the kitchen with my hip, poured the rest of the bourbon into my glass. No ice cubes this time, no water.

There was slightly more than half a glass now.

Back in the chair, then, cushioned comfort, really quite drunk, my head falling to my chest, slugging down big gulps of bourbon. Pure fire. Pure fucking fire, I said out loud.

Took another slug, said, How you like that, motherfucker? to the dark, empty room.

And thought again of all the stupid things I had not done, including the not burning down of the house, driving of the car, kicking of the cats.

Wasn't sure what time it was, but I knew it hadn't been an hour since my first sip, and God, was I drunk. I was totally shitfaced.

Then I wished I had a cigarette. Would kill for a cigarette, even though I hadn't smoked in years.

But right now—damn, a smoke would be good. A smoke would be just perfect. Goes with a drink. Zip and zap.

Deep gulp. Kept gulping. Sucked that glass down like ginger fucking ale.

Whew.

Ice cream.

Piece o cake.

No fucking problem. Lay the glass down on its side on the table. Not break the glass. Careful. Nother thing not do. Burn house. Howl at moon.

Twenty-five years. Crackle and burn.

Slid slow, slid gently to polished wood floor.

Just lay there. So fucking drunk. Shockingly drunk. Hammer blow to back of head. Deeply stupid. Dumb as a bag of dimes. Was this even possible?

Dah dah dah.

Blah de blah da.

Holy shit.

Then in the morning, when the morning came, I was still fairly drunk. Drank orange juice the way I'd had bourbon. Took ibuprofen.

And told Liz about my adventure. Told her some of it. That I'd had a few drinks. That it relaxed me.

I'd been straight and sober many years when we met. She knew nothing about addiction.

I said I thought I'd be having a drink now and then. Because already I was thinking that maybe I could start drinking around noon, maybe by two in the afternoon.

She said, You sure?

Oh yeah, I said. Not a problem.

After a few hours, after most of a bottle of orange juice and several cups of coffee, I went out, bought a bottle of gin, limes and tonic. And for four afternoons and nights I drank, going into deeper and darker and drunker places each time. Places so lightless and loveless and hopeless that there were moments I didn't think I would ever get out.

So I went to a psychiatric unit, where I was admitted and treated for depression. Celexa was switched to Welbutrin, Depakote to Topomax. After five days, the number of days I'd been drinking in all, I left the hospital with prescriptions for a new antidepressant, mood stabilizer, and the name of a new psychiatrist.

Dr. Benz's office was in the east wing of her big, gray stone house, set among trees, flowers, a big gray stone garage, and lots and lots of lawn. The whole neighborhood was big houses on lots of lawn.

The houses said, Look at me.

I did.

Dr. Benz was probably ten years younger than me, had a full head of dark hair, deep brown eyes, a lovely smile. She was warm, smart, empathic, quick.

When I told her about the drinking and the depression, and how now I felt very anxious and pretty depressed, she said, "So drinking's a problem."

"Oh, I'm a full-blown, one hundred and ten percent alcoholic."

She nodded, asked how long that had been going one.

I said, Pretty much my whole life, but just for five days. I'd been clean and sober twenty-five years.

"Congratulations," she said.

She looked down at her notes. She wore a sea-blue silk blouse and black slacks. Her legs were crossed.

"You write books?" she asked. "Novels?"

I nodded.

"What kind of books?"

People always asked me that, and I never knew what to say.

"Literary fiction, I guess. My heroes are Joyce and Faulkner."

"Good heroes." She smiled. "I majored in English at Smith."

I smiled.

"So what do you do for anxiety?"

I shrugged. "Nothing."

"Ever try benzodiazepines?"

"Who?"

"Benzodiazepines."

I shook my head.

"Clonazepam, lorazepam. Ever heard of them?"

"No."

"Klonopin, Ativan, are the brand names. They're relatively new versions of a relatively old drug. An old drug refined."

"And?"

The walls were stacked with books, medical books, psychiatry and psychology books, novels and histories, books on war and trauma.

"They can be very effective against anxiety, even at low doses, and anxiety is one of the major symptoms of depression, a greatly underrated symptom of depression."

I said, Hmmm.

"Well, professor," she said.

"Yes."

She was looking straight at me, smiling, almost melancholy, and I thought, My God, she's gorgeous. Lord, she's kind.

She had an enormous framed degree on the wall from Harvard Medical School. Margaret Joan Benz.

Wow. Fucking Harvard. That was serious.

"Well, doctor," I said. "What do you think?"

She charged one hundred fifty bucks for a half hour.

"I think we should give lorazepam a try. It's fairly short-acting. Clonazepam's more long-acting. We can try you out on a very small dose. A baby dose. Point two-five milligrams, four times a day. To give you an idea how low this dose is, lorazepam comes in point two-five, point five, one and two milligram tablets. So you'll be taking one milligram a day."

She crossed, then recrossed her legs.

Okay, I told her.

Dr. Benz started writing on her prescription pad. Then she handed me the small square of paper. Lorazepam, .25, #124, q.i.d. Four times a day.

I handed her a check.

We made an appointment for the following week.

And a miracle took place, something amazing and transformative. The slow deep grind of anxiety and depression got better, and it got better fast.

I took one little benzo, and I couldn't much tell I'd taken it. This was not like sipping a drink where that powerful warmth, that deep, almost sexual, release happened almost instantly. And then for me a near-instant plunge into drunkenness.

But that constant, tight, tense feeling, the feeling that some-thing really bad was about to happen, the sense that I had done terrible things and would be punished for them—that feeling became less and less strong. And then I didn't notice it at all.

Benzos were the answer. And they didn't mess me up like booze.

When I Googled them, I found out that Librium, the first benzodiazepine, was discovered by Hoffmann-La Roche in 1955. In 1957 Hoffmann-La Roche developed Rohypnol and Valium, and over the years, various companies developed other benzos, including Versed, Mogadon, Prosom, Serax, Halcion, Dalmane, Dormicum, Xanax, Temazepam, Klonopin and Ativan.

They were prescribed for everything from anxiety, insomnia, panic disorder, seizures, and preoperative sedation, to muscle spasms and irritable bowel syndrome.

This went on for four, five, six months. One lorazepam q.i.d. After a few months, just to see what would happen, just to see what it would feel like, I took two tabs instead of one.

And, damn, it felt good. Not like a drink. But the old rule held: If one felt good, two felt better.

Dr. Benz and I were seeing each other every two weeks by then, and after a few months, every month. And I'd save up the pills. Maybe take one in the morning, before teaching, then not take any until the evening. Then in the evening, I'd take three, and that felt good.

Not only was there no anxiety, it was pretty damn relaxing.

Not like booze. Not like booze at all.

In control, and careful. Medical.

So if I was popping a few pills, doctor-sanctioned, Harvard-sanctioned pills, big deal. They weren't fucking my life up like booze. Not even close.

Booze took me down so fast it was not even mildly ambiguous or amusing. Two minutes. Fucking face-flat down. Boom.

I didn't get smashed, blasted, wrecked, or sloppy. Not in the least.

It was just this sweet, slow pleasant buzz.

Liz never knew, the kids never knew. My friends never knew.

My students never knew when I went into my seminars after popping three or four lorazepam and taught—without a trace of tension, anxiety, any of the normal stuff. Just loose and sharp and funny.

And I didn't burn down the house or kick the cats. I didn't stumble when I walked, bump into walls or slur my words.

When I sat down at my computer and Googled clonazepam, I found out that it was pretty similar to lorazepam, only longer-acting, as Dr. Benz had said. And it came in the same strength tablets.

Then I noticed that some of the Google hits said, Buy Clonazepam.

I went from page to page to page.

Wow. Holy shit.

Buy Klonopin. Discount Klonopin. Web Pharmacy. NetRX. Overseas Medicine. Drugs4Sale. Trusted Online RX. International Pharmacy.

There were dozens and dozens of them.

What were these? Where were these? Was this even legal?

It was dark outside my third-floor office. This was well past midnight. The boys and Liz had long since gone to sleep. I pictured Liz in bed, under the covers, reading old copies of *Poetry* magazine, a circle of light over her head. The only light in the office came from the computer. I was so excited I was almost trembling.

Was this possible? Drugs for sale on the Internet?

I clicked on one and it showed a handsome man with horn-rimmed glasses, a white lab coat, a clipboard, looking professional and concerned. Another site had a handsome blonde woman with horn-rimmed glasses, a white lab coat, no clipboard, looking professional and concerned.

I checked an Offshore drug place. Their pharmacist had wire-rimmed glasses, but he did have the white coat and the look of concern.

Under medical problems I clicked Anxiety, and the screen jumped to at least a half-dozen benzos.

They had clonazepam, diazepam, lorazepam, and three or four others. When I clicked on clonazepam, they listed about six options in the number of pills you could order and the strength of the dosage.

You could get thirty one-milligram tablets for about fifty bucks. Sixty for about seventy-five, and so on.

I calculated, and thirty one-milligram tabs was the equivalent of an entire one-hundred-twenty-four tablet supply from Dr. Benz. Her one-month baby dose.

This felt powerful. I could get as many as I wanted.

Fuck Dr. Benz.

Then I saw the two-milligram tablets. You could get one hundred two-milligram tabs for just over a hundred bucks. Plus fifteen dollars shipping.

That was a whole bunch of benzos.

I filled out name and address, a three-question medical information form, which stated that I wanted them for anxiety, that I was six foot one and a half inches, and weighed two-ten, and that my doctor was aware that I was getting this medicine online.

Then I gave them my VISA number.

When I pressed send I only half believed I'd ever get drugs.

Then I stood up, went across the room, and stood against the far wall. I took deep breaths because I was almost shaky. Nervous and excited and scared all at the same time.

I looked the length of the office. Past all the books, the art on the walls, the postcards from friends and students I had tacked up.

There was the deep blue computer screen glowing, and the empty chair with the arms, the high back, just sitting there. Vacated, as though someone should be there but was not.

He was already somewhere else.

He was gone.

11

Morning came slow, and morning came lonely on Men's Primary.

I went back to my bed and lay down. For ten, twenty minutes, maybe a half hour.

I put my head on the pillow, under the pillow, to the side of the pillow. I thought of Liam and Austin, sleeping in their beds, their red hair spread across their pillows like waving tendrils on the floor of the ocean.

They always slept with a leg thrown over the side of the bed, an arm lifted overhead, as though they were dancing or running, as though sleep were an intense, active pursuit.

At home the house was deeply quiet at four-thirty or five in the morning, but by five-thirty Liz's radio-alarm would come on, and she would rise quietly, in the silence, to run on the empty streets and hills of Ithaca.

For five years, right around the time we were having Liam and Austin, I worked as a staff writer for Cornell Magazine, writing feature articles about anything and anyone my editor and I thought were interesting. So I got paid to visit, interview and write about a guy who lost a leg at Normandy; I spent days with a woman who survived Auschwitz; interviewed a man who won the Congressional Medal of Honor in Europe in World War II for acts so brave they were nearly insane. I shadowed a dairy farmer for a fifteen-hour-day in October, the leaves the color of fire, and when I asked him when he last took a vacation he said, "Oh, my wife and I took Christmas off seven, eight years ago."

I got to walk around the deserted halls of the buildings of a giant state mental institution, because very briefly, for one year, it had started out as Cornell University, and on the wall in a former ward was a crayon drawing. It looked like a child's drawing: a blue lake, sky, yellow sun, a bird flying. Then when I looked closer I saw the fine mesh on the whole front of the drawing. I looked up and out the window.

And there it was—the whole drawing the way a patient must have seen it. All but the bird. Lake, sky, sun, mesh covering the window.

I wrote the article about Willard State Hospital, and we put it on the cover of our next issue. We called it "Asylum."

I turned onto my stomach, my side, my back, said, God Help, ten or twenty times, then knew there would be no more sleep.

So I got up, brushed my teeth, looked at my jungle hair in the mirror, went out to the lounge.

It was four-fifty-three.

Nobody ever died for lack of sleep. Or so somebody said.

Fuck it. And fuck this. And fuck that. And fuck the rest of everything.

One of my favorite friends, Knocko of Boston, used to joke that he was going to write his autobiography and call it, Fuck Ya, Fuck All Of Yez.

And fuck Caron too, I thought.

Out in the dark lounge, Levon, Chuck and Doc were sitting and laughing, talking in low voices.

"You sleep?" Doc asked.

"Hour and a half, two hours," I said. "You?"

"Same," he said, then started to laugh, an almost crazy full laugh.

Doc was wearing dark dress pants, a blue Oxford shirt, and black loafers. Put a tie on him, and he could start seeing patients. Give him the white lab coat, the professional and concerned look, and he could start billing people.

"Hey Doc," I said. "What's a smart guy like you doing in a dump like this?"

Doc started laughing his crazy wonderful laugh.

"What about you, professor?" Chuck said. "Know what I'm saying."

We all laughed, and nothing was even funny.

"Fucking five in the morning," Chuck said.

"Faculty lounge," Levon said. "Doctor's lounge."

A short round guy with a Mohawk came out of the C.A.'s office.

"Jimmy," Levon and Chuck said.

Jimmy was smiling.

"You guys aren't supposed to be laughing," he said. "Against the rules."

"Is that for right now, or all day and night?" Levon asked.

"All day and night," Jimmy said.

"Jimmy," Chuck said, "Doc was just getting ready to write us scripts. Nothing serious, just stuff to take the edge off and help us get a little sleep."

"And maybe a little get-up in the morning," Levon said. "You know how those mornings can be?"

Everyone was giggling. Cackling.

We were in junior high. We were in grade school.

"You know what, guys?" Jimmy said. "I know this kind of sucks. All of you are going through detox, through withdrawal, and you're all hitting the wall, and no matter what we do that's not gonna feel good.

"But I love to hear you laugh. Just laugh and laugh. Because that's what makes you heal."

We didn't laugh.

We sat in the quiet, and around the edge of the curtains the dark was turning less dark, was becoming faintly gray.

The eight-thirty lecture was about the first step. We admitted we were powerless over alcohol and that our lives had become unmanageable.

"Notice the first word," the counselor woman, Sandy, said. Tan hair, lean, middle-aged, glasses hanging from her neck by a black cord. Ironic. Edgy.

"We hold these truths to be self-evident," Doc whispered. He was sitting and shaking between me and Bert. Bert's belly stuck out halfway to the seat in front of him.

"Shut the fuck up," Bert said.

Doc and I wore coats, Bert had on a bright, plaid, short-sleeved shirt.

"That all men are created equal," I whispered.

I held my hand out in front of me, fingers spread, and my fingers were trembling.

"Fucking Yankees," Bert drawled.

This was junior high. People looked at us.

"Gentlemen," Sandy said.

Bert looked to his left and right. People laughed.

"We," Doc said in an official doctor voice. "It's a we program."

"And why's that, Devin?"

Sandy wasn't going to call him Doctor. In here he had no authority.

"Because we can't do this alone."

"Very good, Devin."

"Thank you," he said. Doc sat up straight. He beamed.

Sandy said that whether we knew it or not, we wouldn't be sitting in here, in Caron, in Chit Chat Auditorium, listening to her on a Friday morning, at this hour, if we weren't powerless over alcohol or some other drug.

She paced as she talked and seemed to fix her attention, moment by moment, on individuals in the audience. I was afraid she would stop and call on me.

"How many of you can think of things you'd rather be doing right now?" she asked. "Places you'd rather be?"

Sandy raised her own hand.

Nobody moved.

"None of you. Ha. C'mon. We're supposed to be getting honest."

A few hands went up, then more and more.

"A wine and candlelight dinner with that special someone. A great movie with that other special someone. A beach with white sand and deep aqua-blue water. Cutting lines of coke. Washing down some vikes with a cold cold beer."

Everyone's hand was up.

"Good," she said. "You wouldn't be human, or an addict, if there wasn't at least part of you that wanted to be somewhere else."

She turned, paced, looked at the back wall.

"And I can think of plenty of places and things that might be just a little bit more fun than seeing your smiling faces at eight-thirty on Friday morning."

She looked from one side of the aisle to the other.

"But you know what? I'm honest to God glad to be here. Happy to be here. Lucky to be here."

Sandy was powerless over alcohol. And drugs. And sex. And gambling. And shopping. And a lot of things.

My God, her life was so fucked up, so unmanageable and trashed and catastrophic, it was on the I.C.U. It had so many tubes and lines running out of every orifice, limb, joint and inch of skin that there was very little hope of anything.

When she used the word unmanageable, did any of us have any idea what she was talking about? Anything come to mind? Anything specific?

"Vomit," someone said.

"Jail."

"Car crashes."

"Tears."

"Lies."

"Debt."

Sandy said, "Yes, yes, yes, yes, yes, yes."

So when Sandy said she could think of many many attractive alternatives to being here right now, being here helped her stay straight and sober, and being here kept it green, kept it fresh, reminded her of what it was like to be an active alcoholic and addict, and the vomit, tears, car crashes, lies, debt, and absolute misery of that disease when it's active. She felt lucky and grateful to be here with us.

"Because like it or not, people, we—and I emphasize we—are in this together, and I can't do it without you."

Then her voice got soft.

"And I'm deeply, honestly moved, honored and moved, to see each one of you begin this journey. Because what's more remarkable than saving a human life? And make no mistake: that's what each of you is doing."

There was only fifteen minutes to have a smoke then get up to the meat locker for small group.

Small group, Raphael said, was kind of the big meeting each day. Maybe ten or twelve guys, and two counselors, in the windowless room, for an hour and a quarter.

"No break?" I asked.

Raphael laughed.

"No break, dude. So get your cigs in now."

The bell tower clock said nine-thirty-four, and there had to be twenty-five guys smoking, laughing, looking at trees, at sky, kicking gravel, talking, not listening.

Raphael was a grade school teacher in Baltimore, and when I asked what was his drug of choice had been he said, "Crack."

I said, "Wow."

Then I asked what made him stop.

"I ran out of money," he said.

I just looked at him. Just looked and looked.

Someone said, "Time."

Ten or twelve chairs in the meat locker were arranged in a tight oval, and the lights were bright.

The two counselors were Bowtie and Stan, who had black hair, very pale skin, and bad allergies. His face was red from sneezing and sniffling, his dark eyes watered.

Stan wore a long, metallic gray tie on a black shirt, and though he had big shoulders and arms, he had tiny hands and feet. He and Bowtie sat with one empty chair between them near the eraser boards at the front of the room. Bowtie's bowtie was big and bright. His posture was perfect. He looked like he could take out a small infantry platoon.

Guys dripped in. There were sixteen of us, including the counselors. Both counselors had pens and clipboards. And there were exactly sixteen chairs in the oval.

Alan closed the door, and there was a tight, sealed feel to the room. Meat locker indeed.

"How you guys doing today?" Stan asked. He looked around the room.

Bowtie looked around the room.

Many of the guys looked around the room.

Most were sitting with their ankles on their knees, guy-style, a few, including me and Stan and Max, had our legs crossed knee to knee, and a small good-looking guy was sitting cross-legged, half-lotus.

"Don't all answer at once," Stan said, and laughed loud and hard, the sound banging off the walls.

"Toby?" Bowtie said.

"Able to be up and around."

"Well, shit, we expect that much," Bowtie said.

"Tim?" Stan asked.

Tim nodded. He was wearing his leather jacket.

"You speak with your mother?" Bowtie asked.

"Yeah," Tim said.

"How'd that go?"

Tim nodded.

Stan and Bowtie kept looking us over. I felt Stan's dark eyes on me.

"Paul," he said. "I'm Stan, and I'm your counselor. Welcome."

We leaned across the oval and shook hands.

"After group let's set up a time to meet in my office, okay?"

I nodded.

Stan cleared his throat. "Once again, welcome to small group. Paul is just up from detox, so welcome to Paul. Maybe we can go around the room, introduce ourselves, say where we're from, name your drug of choice, and that sort of thing."

Everyone did that, and the only one I didn't know was the good-looking lotus guy. He was Bobby and he was from Washington D.C., and he was a pills and booze person.

After each person named their drug of choice, Max repeated it, with energy. If someone said, Pills and booze, Max said, Oh man, Pills and booze! Or, heroin and percs, Max said, HEROIN AND PERCS.

Max kind of jerked and jumped in his chair.

"Okay," Bowtie said when we finished. "Let's try again. How's everyone doing this morning?"

Max said, "I just want to welcome our distinguished new visitor, a published author, a veritable wordsmith, into our midst."

Doc cleared his throat.

"Not to mention our distinguished physician."

"Aw, fuck, man," Bert said.

"Wait a second, Bert," Stan said.

"Bunch of distinguished fucking addicts," Levon said.

The room roared, laughing. Two guys slapped their thighs. Arnold half fell from his chair.

"Gentlemen," Bowtie said.

"Who?" Bobby asked.

"A gentle-what?"

"A ga-who?"

"You know him?" Marcel asked me.

"Guys," Stan and Bowtie said.

"Fucking hammerheads," Alan said.

Bobby was two seats over. He looked at me, grinned and said, "How do you like us so far?"

Then I started laughing.

"As I was saying," Max said.

"Guys," Stan said.

"Gentlemen," Bowtie said.

"As I was saying," Max said again.

"Max," someone said. Then someone else said, "Max."

"It's a distinct pleasure to welcome new faces, and prepare to say goodbye to the old." He looked at Ricky.

"Ricky," several people said.

Ricky raised his fist, circled it in the air.

It reminded him of his own first days on the unit, not so long ago, Max began, when he was fresh from the hospital and pretty darn shaky and not sure at all which way he was going, up or down or sideways or under, for that matter.

We go down this path with alcohol and drugs, and by God, we honestly had no idea where that path was going to take us, what darker, lesser paths there would be, and how the light would give way to the dark.

"This path going anywhere?" Marcel whispered, and I did my best not to laugh.

And so you're on this path, Max said, and it put him in mind of the great Italian poet, who said, In the middle of the journey through my life I awoke and found myself lost in a dark wood. Or something like that.

"Christ," Bert said. "An eye-tie."

"Guys," Stan said.

I couldn't help myself. "Dante," I said.

Max smiled big.

"Finally some learning in these unlettered halls," he said. "Thank you, professor."

Max said, "May I continue?"

Bowtie nodded, Marcel hissed, "Kiss-ass," and I gave him a barely concealed finger.

"So a man journeys along, not knowing of course that his trials, his tribulations are as perilous, nay, more perilous than those of wily Odysseus."

Did he say nay? Did he really say nay?

"He meets his own one-eyed giants. His own Sirens calling him to the rocks."

Why the fuck had I encouraged him?

"Motherfucker," Chuck said loudly, under his breath.

"And all he wants to do is get home. Or so it seems," Max said. "The place of warmth and comfort, of familiar faces, a hug, a kiss."

"A wide-screen television," Toby said.

"Six-pack of frosties in the fridge," Levon said.

"Fuck that," Chuck said. "Bags of dope, clean needles, cell phone. Know what I'm saying."

"Why am I continually surrounded by Philistines?" Max asked.

"By who?" Arnold asked.

"People from Philly," Bobby said.

"What the fuck's it mean?" Bert asked. He looked at me.

Bowtie looked at me.

"An uncultured, materialistic person," I said.

"Dude," a few people said.

"Motherfucker," Bert said.

"What did I say about distinguished?" Max asked.

"You can go fuck yourself, you meth-head motherfucking philly-stine," Bert said. "Cause you didn't ride in here on a white fucking horse even though you act like you done."

Everyone was screaming laughing. Alan, Chuck and Marcel were leaning so far over to the side, their chairs were on two legs, and Toby was ready to topple backwards.

Stan and Bowtie were laughing hard too.

"So as I was saying," Max tried to continue, "the path can take us to many surprising places."

"Like the fucking meat locker at Caron," Arnold said, which brought on still more laughter.

Max stood up, and everyone watched him but kept laughing.

"The back seat of Sticks' Chevy," Chuck said.

"So if you'll all excuse me," Max said. He turned and left.

People were wiping their eyes. They were adjusting their shirts and belt buckles.

"Anybody care to check on Max?" Stan asked.

Raphael got up and left.

"So," Bowtie said.

There was quiet, deep quiet, as though the teacher had returned after the spitball fight.

"I'm sorry," Bert said. "That was rude and crude, but the motherfucker is a motherfucker."

More quiet.

"Anyone else?" Stan asked.

"He's a dick," Bobby said.

"No, a prick," Alan said.

"But we are Philistines," Doc said. "He got that right."

"Does any of this have anything to do with addiction?" Stan asked.

"Sure," Doc said.

Arnold blinked, shifted in his seat, licked his dry lips. He looked as though he'd been hit on the head with a shovel. "I think so."

"We don't know when to stop," Toby said.

"We push and push and push till things are way the fuck out of control," Alan said.

Guys were looking at their sneakers and knees and walls. Nobody was looking at anybody else.

"Then what happens?"

"Fucking joy," Bert said.

Bowtie said, "Joy. Interesting word. Say more."

"Like getting fucking drunk, snorting lines of coke," Bert said.

"Jamming dope," Chuck said. "Feels really really really good. Unbelievable."

"For how long."

"Till it doesn't," Ricky said.

Raphael came back. "Can't find him."

"Feels good till the next shot, next drink, next pill," Chuck said.

"Always chasing it," Levon said.

"Chasing what?" Stan asked.

Some quiet, some silence, only people were looking at each other. People were thinking.

Finally Doc said, "The high and the joy. The promise of something."

Bowtie asked, "What does it promise you? Jelly beans? A hundred grand a year for life? A bucket of shit a day?"

"The bucket, man," Bert said. "I'd say the bucket for sure."

Stan laughed the big laugh.

"That's what you get," Bert said, "but that ain't the promise."

"Cause if that was the promise," Bowtie said, "you wouldn't go for it, would you?" He looked at me. "Paul, I got a bucket of shit, and I can guarantee you one just like this every day. You interested?"

"I don't think so," I said.

"Why not?" he asked. "Any takers? Tim? Bobby? Raphael? Doc? Nice warm steaming shit? All yours, gentleman. I promise."

"C'mon, guys," Stan said. "It's free. This is a solemn promise." He leaned over and slapped Bowtie's big shoulder.

"But you know what?" Bowtie said. "You do it every day you use." He looked slowly from face to face to face to face.

"Cause it whispers to you. It's gonna kiss you and lick you and make you feel really fucking good."

"Sex," Tim said.

"Give you a big fucking hardon," Bobby said.

"Cock tease."

Guys were nodding. Guys were smiling, and then they were not smiling.

"Then it flicks the lights on," Bowtie said, "and you're in bed with a hag, with a real scary witch, and she's covered in sores, and she's got pus oozing from every pore, and she's not there to give you pleasure. She's there to fuck you up."

He kept looking around the room, and Stan was looking around the room, and almost everybody else was staring at the carpet hard. Stan had clear brown eyes behind big-rimmed glasses. He looked at me, then he looked at Marcel.

"So where's Max?" Stan asked.

People were very quiet.

"My fault," Bert said.

"Never mind fault," Bowtie said. "Where is he?"

"Maybe we could go look," Doc said.

"Maybe that's an idea," Bowtie said.

12

D ay six on Men's Primary and my detox protocol had changed. I was down to two 1 m.g. tabs of Ativan a day, one at breakfast, one at bedtime, and withdrawal was getting worse by the day, the feeling of estrangement, the jerking and trembling, the sleep, now down to maybe an hour a night. Dr. Troncale said it was going to get better, but it was going to take a while, and he wished he could tell me how long a while. Days, weeks, months, possibly years. It was a nasty, tricky withdrawal. That's all he could tell me for sure.

"Sooner or later," he said, "you've gotta walk through the wall."

My memory was slightly better than a week earlier, but I still called people by the wrong name, and had to pull a copy of the Patient Schedule from my pocket ten times a day to tell where I was supposed to be.

Tim, Ricky and Raphael had graduated, Ricky and Raphael to group residences, Tim to his own home, where everyone expected him to resume drinking pretty quickly.

"He'll be one dead motherfucker inside a month," Bert said.

"Mr. Compassion," Levon said.

"Just speaking it like I see it," Bert said.

The day Tim went out to drink and die or live and flourish, a bent-over man in his seventies, named Judd, whom Bert christened "Old Dude," came in. He wore a white tee-shirt, blue and white checked pajama bottoms, and was very thin. He walked at a slant as though he was about to fall over, and he flossed his teeth constantly, dropping his floss wherever he happened to be, whenever he happened to be done.

Judd had gorgeous brown eyes, and when he smiled, which wasn't often, his face was a thousand watts.

Rumor was that before he came to Caron, 1.7 million dollars in cash was found in his house in Pittsburgh. Not two million or a million and a half, but 1.7 million. It was that kind of exactitude, that detail, that made us believe.

He was also seriously addicted to Percocet and OxyContin, pain pills he'd started taking after several surgeries. He was some kind of dealer in used car parts. The biggest in Pittsburgh, he told Alan. He also told Levon he was a tough old Jew. A mean son of a bitch.

Despite the 1.7 million, Judd had no money in here. So he was always bumming cigarettes. But he wouldn't speak much at first, so he didn't say, "Can I've a smoke?" He went up to you, put two fingers to his lips and you just handed one over.

I'd given him a half dozen smokes and he hadn't once said thanks. So out at the Butt Hut, when he did the finger to lips routine, I gave him one, was about to say something sarcastic about manners and gratitude, when he poked me gently in the stomach with his forefinger by way of thanks.

Sweet old dude, I thought.

Later that night, the C.A. Matthew came into the lounge swearing. He was at the end of his shift, was about to leave for home, and he'd caught Old Dude at the Butt Hut with a cell phone, placing bets on the basketball playoffs with his bookie. Both of which were against every rule in the house.

A fucking cell phone!

Fucking bets!

So Matthew had to confiscate the cell phone, and Matthew had to stay an extra hour and fill out a detailed Incident Report.

Guys on the Unit, guys on D-Block, as we liked to call ourselves, were shocked and delighted and outraged, all at the same time.

But two days after Judd came in, a coke-head named Edmund arrived. He was from Ohio, was short and solidly built, had merry eyes, and almost never stopped talking.

Edmund owned a company that did large computer systems for institutions, small governments, colleges, hospitals, and he had also done stand-up comedy.

Out at the Butt Hut, on Edmund's first night, Judd made the mistake of pulling his wallet from his pajama pocket and showing photos of his alleged girlfriend, who was naked, and looked, Edmund said, like an eighteen-year-old Russian gymnast.

I didn't look because I didn't want to be tormented by such sights, just as I wouldn't want to see a bottle of Valium. Guys crowded around.

"How old is she, Judd?" Edmund asked.

"Twenty-two," he said in his tough-guy gravel voice.

Guys hooted and laughed, slapped each other on the arms and backs.

"How old're you?" Bert asked.

"Seventy-three."

"What's she see in you?" Edmund asked.

"I got a nine-inch prick," he said. He wasn't smiling. He seemed to expect people to believe him.

The laughter was wild. The laughter hit trees, it hit the walls of the building which was thirty yards away. People had tears in their eyes, they were bent over.

Edmund had the face of a funeral director. But his eyes did a tango. The lights made crazy shadows on his face in the night.

"How tall're you, Judd?" Edmund asked. "Give or take a few inches."

"Five-five."

"How much you weigh?"

"One-twenty-two."

"So you get a woody on, that's a big percentage of your body weight?"

Judd was smiling.

"Do the math, my friend," Judd said.

"All the blood rushing down there at once, that must make you light-headed," Edmund said.

Guys were howling, holding their middles to stop from peeing.

"Not to mention the weight."

My jaws hurt. I was crying. Everything hurt from laughing.

"Stop, Eddie," people cried. "Eddie, Jesus."

"The weight would just pull you forward, do a face plant, just drill the floor with that thing."

Under the hoots and howls, Judd said, "You got it, you use it."

"You gotta register something that big? That dangerous?"

"Shit, shit," guys were saying.

Judd sat and smiled.

"Liable to maim or kill that poor girl."

Dave, the C.A., came out and said, "You guys, you fucking guys."

Judd flicked his cigarette into the middle of the oval of chairs. He started to get up, fell back down, then got up again, pulled floss from a pocket, and started flossing his teeth.

"The other great thing, Judd, a real fucking community service you do for us," Edmund said, "is these used pieces of floss all over the place. We don't have to ask you what you had for dinner, and it's never a fucking mystery what they served down at the cafeteria. We just look down at one of your flosses and there's all the information we need."

Judd stood and smiled and flossed.

"So thanks for thinking of us."

More howling. A river of antic addict laughter.

When things had quieted a little, Judd said, "You're welcome." Then he dropped his floss and walked slowly and at a slant toward the building. Because of the angle of the light, his shadow was at least nine slanted feet tall.

Twenty-two years old and I had not gone to college, and I hadn't had many jobs, and I lived in my parents' house. I read all the time, and did lots of writing, and I honest-to-God thought I was a mental case, a crazy person. Because very weird shit took place all the time. Terrible, black and paralyzing depression, and wild happy weeks of energy and sleeplessness and work, and anxiety so intense, so powerful, leading me to dark, closed spaces that I never wanted to leave.

There was a dapper psychiatrist named Covern who had a long brown coat with a fur collar. He had gone to Harvard—fucking Harvard again—and he was always tapping pencils and paper clips on the desktop.

Covern was small and elfin. He had a smile that was hard to read.

He had a big private practice, and I saw him at the outpatient clinic at the local hospital, for maybe five, reduced bucks a session.

When I heard about the big private practice, I said to him, "So you coming here and seeing me for almost nothing, you're slumming."

"Why're you a slum?" Covern asked.

Mostly we talked about drugs, and he'd write me scripts almost upon request. I'd heard about the major tranquilizers, the anti-psychotics, such as Thorazine, Stelazine, Mellaril, and the big one, Haldol. I'd request Thorazine, try it for a few weeks or a month, then switch to Stelazine.

I was hoping for tranquility, for some relief from the emotional drama, but instead of anything resembling tranquility, these drugs would subdue you, tie you up and put you in a glass or steel or concrete room and lock the door. And you'd sit soundlessly inside, with a kind of muted agitation that made you want to—but unable to—scream.

After about six months of major tranquilizers, I began to take Valium and Librium instead, and felt better fast.

After a year of seeing Covern, I came to an appointment drunk. I was sloppy and silly and stupid.

He kept looking down and smoothing his tie, brushing nothing from its silk front, flipping the tie up, his face getting more and more red and more elfin.

"What'd you drink?" he asked.

"Beer."

"How much?"

"Lots of fucking beer."

He said it was an outrage to show up for an appointment drunk. It was thoughtless, it was disrespectful.

"It was drunk," I said, which I considered witty, and I began to giggle.

"Enough of this, enough of you. You're an alcoholic, mister."

Mister!

He stood up, and that was the end of my time with Covern.

Then I began going to four or five different doctors, complaining of migraines, insomnia, anxiety. I always wore an Oxford shirt, chinos, penny-loafers, horn-rimmed glasses. I looked pretty good and sounded pretty good. I didn't look or sound like a drug addict.

I had a rap about the aura of the migraine, how painful light and sound were, the vomiting, the ice packs on my head.

As with many things, there was at least some truth to what I said. At least some. I did get bad headaches, and I did have awful anxiety and insomnia. But I wasn't even sure if I believed my own bullshit. That was one of the scariest things. Not knowing what the truth was, or if a little truth could be stretched into a half or whole truth.

Many of my symptoms came directly from drinking and drug use. They were fucking me up in large ways. But the booze and drugs seemed also to offer the only temporary relief from the symptoms.

I got prescriptions for Fiorinal with codeine, for Valium, for a benzo called Dalmane, which was supposed to help with sleep. Each script was for fifty or eighty or a hundred pills, and each had three or four refills. I went to four different pharmacies, and kept track of the doctors, the pharmacies and refills in a small red notebook.

This was the best and the worst scenario. More pills than I could want.

The scenario got deeper and darker.

My father would stand in the doorway of my bedroom and ask if I was okay, if there was anything he could do. I'd say I was fine. Honest. I was okay.

By the early summer when I was twenty-two, I weighed one-hundred-thirty-two pounds, and my brother Shawn found me crouching in the closet of my bedroom at my parents' house. When he asked me what I was doing, he said I said that the CIA was after me. I have no memory of being in the closet or of saying any such thing, but he swears I did.

I refused to get in a car and go to a hospital, so my parents did the only thing they could do. They called the cops on me.

So two big guys arrived into the little world of my room, a place of books, music, art posters on the wall, a place of drugs.

They had the big cop belts with handcuffs, nightsticks, radios and guns, but they didn't need any of that.

In the back seat of the cruiser, I bummed a smoke from the guy riding shotgun, and he even lit it for me and handed it back through the heavy grill.

At the hospital emergency ward, the same hospital where I'd seen Covern, an intern, a skinny guy with glasses and all the answers, ordered that I be given a shot of Haldol, the major anti-psychotic tranquilizer.

I asked him not to, said that I was allergic to Haldol, that I'd have a dystonic reaction, which were these weird muscular reactions that resembled the snake-like movements of Parkinson's Disease. It had happened to me before.

But he gave me the shot, I had the dystonic reaction, he looked alarmed, and I said I needed a shot of Cogentin to counteract the Haldol. He said he had to call the senior physician.

It took an hour to get in touch with the senior physician, then he ordered Cogentin. As soon as the intern gave it to me, the dystonic reaction stopped. I stood up and punched the intern.

Within twenty minutes I was in a straightjacket, with a pink paper, a thirty-day commitment, on my way to a state mental hospital.

Medfield State was about twenty miles southwest of Boston and had dozens and dozens of red, two-story brick buildings spread over hundreds of acres. There was a big rusting water tower on a hill, a newer administration building near the front of the grounds. Ward R-2, where I was sent, was on the second floor of a building at the back of the grounds.

Martin Scorcese's *Shutter Island* was filmed at Medfield.

They put my name on the board in the nurses' office, with the initials HP and SP next to it. I asked what that meant and they said, Homicide Precautions and Suicide Precautions.

"Hit someone here," a nurse in a red cardigan said, "and you'll be in Bridgewater within an hour."

Bridgewater was the state hospital for the criminally insane. If someone took an axe and slaughtered their family at three in the morning, they were sent to Bridgewater. It's where Albert DiSalvo, the Boston Strangler, had been kept.

Heavy black mesh covered the windows in every room. The patients wore slippers and pajama bottoms. I paced the long white halls with them, hung out, felt the drugs seep from my system.

A tall woman with crazy gray hair swore that someone was sneaking into her bed at night, trying to violate her. A big man with a dark unshaven face barely moved, scarcely seemed to blink or breathe. His name was Wayne and he had been in the hospital thirty or forty times over the years.

A young fat guy named Lincoln had deep yellow stains from cigarettes on his right hand.

He had so much money hidden away, he whispered, that when he got out he was going to buy and sell the whole fucking hospital, five times over.

"You think I won't? You think I won't?" he said to a smirking woman in a flowered housedress.

"Fuck," she said. "Fuck fuck fuck."

On Men's Primary, late in the afternoon on day six, the guys were saying, "Fuck, dude. Fuck, man."

I wondered aloud what would happen if we eliminated the word "fuck" from our vocabularies.

"Fuck, professor," Bert said. "What're you talking about?"

"Our conversations would go down by half, immediately."

"But we'd lose the best fucking word in the language," Chuck said.

"Nah," Alan said. "There's way better words."

"Fuck, what?" Bert said. "Name a better fucking word."

Alan said, "Oak."

All around the Butt Hut guys said, "Oak? Oak? The fuck?"

"Hemlock," Alan said. "Sunrise."

"Lovely's lovely," I said.

"Ah fuck," about five guys said. "Lovely?"

Levon took a pull on his smoke and said, "Dappled."

"You Yankee dicks," Bert said. "Motherfuckers."

Levon said, "Ignorant, sister-fucking hick. Those are good ones."

"Beach," Billy said.

"Breast," Edmund said.

"Pickup truck," Toby said, and everyone howled.

Pickup truck?

"Chainsaw," Alan said.

Doc said Ambien sounded damn good sometimes.

Coke.

Kipp said, "Nothing."

Nothing?

"As in negation," Kipp said.

Molson.

Arnold said, "Manhattan," and Marcel wanted to know if he meant the place or the drink.

"How about a Manhattan in Manhattan," Arnold said.

Arnold was still snowed most of the time, but there were small improvements day by day, more words, less sleep during meetings and lectures, fewer bumps against walls.

The previous day, playing volleyball at the gym, Arnold had lifted his hands to hit the ball. He missed entirely, but the ball bounced off his forehead and over the net for a point.

Guys were mentioning other words, mostly sex, drinking and drug-related, when two guys came up the road with Kevin, everyone's favorite C.A.

Kevin had this kind of glow about him that you'd sometimes see in people from AA. Kevin walked with a limp, as though he'd had hip replacement surgery that went bad.

He had sharp features, bright green eyes.

Kevin, along with another C.A. named Len, were the two staff people who went into town to buy cigarettes for patients. Both were scrupulous about the orders. They always returned with your smokes in a plastic bag, a receipt, and if there was fourteen cents change, the fourteen cents was in the bottom of the bag, to the penny.

Kevin was fair, human, humble, strong. He'd been straight and sober something like twenty years, and he had the serenity people talked about in AA, a calm that seemed almost Buddhist. As though he'd found and lived in "the still point in the turning world."

The two guys with him—both patients by the shuffle, the tremor, the dazed look in their eyes—were hauling luggage. A little balding guy with odd facial tics was carrying a green trash bag over his shoulder. He wore a blaze-red jacket, sweatpants, and giant K-Mart basketball sneakers, though he didn't look as though he had ever played.

The other guy was in his mid-sixties, wore a blue blazer, a bright orange polo shirt, and pulled a black leather suitcase.

He had a big distinguished nose, half glasses, and walked stiffly and slowly, like he'd been beaten up.

Kevin walked between the two of them, talking and smiling, as if these were his best friends in the world. And in that moment, of course, they were. Kevin would have said that these two guys were just a couple of drunks, like himself.

They stopped, and fifteen or twenty guys crowded around.

"This is Davy," Kevin said, indicating the little guy, who up close seemed even stranger.

His tongue seemed to snake around in his mouth, and his eyes rolled up every few minutes. His head moved from side to side involuntarily.

Davy nodded, looked nervous, and as people shook his hand, patted his arm and back, said their name, he was silent. He just smiled, made his small movements.

"And Matthias," Kevin said.

Matthias said, "Gentlemen."

"Counselor," Kevin added.

"The fuck?" Bobby said.

"Counselor," Kevin repeated.

"Ignorant," said Kipp.

"What'd you say about me?" Bert said.

Chuck said, "Forget it, big guy."

I couldn't stop myself.

"Counselor means he's a lawyer," I said.

"Motherfucker," Edmund said, and Doc said, "Don't you remember we agreed not to use the word fuck?"

Everyone started yelling at the same time. Fuck this, fuck that, fuck your sister and your sister's brother. Fuck Caron.

"Except you, Kevin," Toby said.

Kipp said he was so glad to be leaving, he couldn't wait to get the fuck out of there, away from these crazy motherfuckers. It was like living in a fraternity house.

A chunky guy from Relapse named Albert asked him when he was taking off.

He said he had a ride from Caron at two, taking him to the airport in Philly for his flight at four-thirty.

You gonna be okay? Jake asked.

"Fuck yeah," Kipp said.

"Dude's huge," someone said, in a voice none of us had heard before. A full rich voice.

"Dude's huge," Davy said again, and he was looking at Jake.

Davy was saying exactly what every one of us thought when we first saw Jake.

Jake was looking at Davy, and he was smiling big.

The next morning was clear, the sky deep blue, the air sparkling.

On the way up from breakfast, something was going on. Some buzz, some something in the air along the road from the cafeteria.

People were gathered in groups all along the small road.

Guys, women, staff, in threes, fives, in one group that might have had a dozen people.

People wearing sweats and sneakers, the women wearing earrings and necklaces, even at this hour.

"Dead," I heard. "Stone-cold, D.O.A. dead."

Albert was sobbing and sobbing, his face contorted so that I almost didn't recognize him. A woman in white, with black hair, had her arm around him. For once, staff did not separate the man and the woman.

Jake was standing alone, his eyes shiny.

When I went up to him, he grabbed and hugged me. It was like being hugged by a tree.

"What, Jake?"

"Kipp's dead."

He went to the airport, went to the bar as soon as the driver dropped him off. Then he got a room, got bottles.

Went home. Got more bottles. Stayed in his room.

He drank and he drank and he drank.

Alcohol poisoning. A severe assault to the brain.

Body found this morning.

Kipp gone.

I thought, Hemlock. Sunrise. Dappled.

Like poison. Like day. Like light.

13

T he first time I saw my son Liam run in a cross-country meet he was a high school sophomore, in a town about thirty miles from Ithaca. A damp misty day in October, huge green fields, enormous trees in full gold and orange and red foliage, and maybe two hundred kids in equally bright colors lined up along one side of the field.

I thought I'd lose him in the crowd, but I didn't.

He was tall, had that long red hair to his shoulders, and he was wearing a maroon warm-up suit.

On the starting line he looked intense, looked serious as a heart attack. He took off the suit, and his arms and legs were long and muscular and very white.

He looked like somebody else, like someone I almost didn't know.

He was in the middle of a group of maybe ten teammates, all of them wearing maroon tops and shorts.

Then the whole line of runners grew still, silent, and far across the field a man in a blaze-orange vest barked, "Ready," and they crouched.

He raised his arm, pistol in hand.

"Set."

Bang.

And they went.

Liam was all power, fluid motion, he was long and white, and he was very fast.

With maybe ten other runners he went quickly to the front of the pack of two hundred and he was some other kid, some other Liam, someone so good at this that by the end of his sophomore season he was made captain of the cross-country team.

And when Austin sang, in the high school auditorium, where they had moved the concert because the middle school did not have an auditorium big enough, he was tall too, and his hair was the same shade of red.

He wore black pants and a white shirt, and there had to be eighty or a hundred kids on stage, and close to a thousand people in the audience.

Austin had performed several solos in the past. He was in an all-county choir, an all-regional choir, and he had a voice that was astonishing.

He stepped off the risers, moved forward, stood alone, and the conductor raised his arm.

Austin opened his mouth, lifted his voice, went high, went low, went over and in and through.

With such power, delicacy, warmth, sweetness.

His voice filled the big room, and it was no voice I'd heard, it was a voice that had nothing to do with me.

Standing in the bathroom at Caron, staring in the mirror, I was someone I didn't know, didn't recognize.

This shaky, shaken man. Straight man. Addict. Person in withdrawal. Person with a disease in remission.

He was some guy who was from somewhere, and he was no doubt going somewhere, but not at the moment. For now he was only for now.

Just here, just now.

So Chapel. Sunday morning Chapel.

They had to be kidding.

First Sunday on the Unit I blew it off. But you had to go to some spiritual something, so I went to a spiritual discussion with all the other atheists in a conference room.

What did spirit mean?

Nobody knew.

Creatures in white sheets.

Men and women with harps.

Hard liquor. Wine and spirits.

The woman leading the discussion was about fifty, had frosted hair, seemed tired. From looking for the spirit?

I looked around the room. Thirty or so guys, every one a drunk and addict with a banged-up brain, just days out of detox, shaking. Could we know anything about the spirit? Could we know quite a bit?

But all week people were talking about Chapel, Chapel.

Father Bill, they said. Fucking A. Father Bill.

Even the most hardened criminals liked Father Bill.

"Listen," Levon said. "Check it out. Get there early. Standing room only."

Plus it was a big AA step: "Made a decision to turn our will and our lives over to the care of God as we understood Him."

Like this disease was a fucker. A killer.

I knew I had the disease, knew I needed help. Couldn't get well on my own. I tried so long.

Maybe something outside of me could help. Whatever it was, no matter what it was called.

And this Father Bill guy. Who cared if he was a priest?

Levon was at least half Jewish, for God's sake.

Eight-fifteen Sunday morning, Memorial Day weekend, I was sitting next to Levon in Chit Chat, and the place was two-thirds full, the place was crackling already.

People kept coming in, and there was loud, happy music on the sound system, and because we never heard music, not ever, it sounded good. I felt like dancing.

There he was up front, talking to people, hugging, listening, lots of hands on faces, arms, backs.

Father Bill.

Levon had told me some about him.

That he was in his late seventies, was a former Marine chaplain who had served in Vietnam, that he was one of us, an addict and alcoholic, but sober close to forty years. And he'd been at Caron a long time, many decades.

They had an altar up front, but sitting on the front of the altar were stuffed animals, wind-up toys, cards and paintings and letters.

In the first few rows were boys and girls from the adolescent units, kids between fifteen and their early twenties. I kept looking at them and looking at them, amazed by how young they looked. Then I found myself fighting tears, and I thought, That's me, forty years ago.

That's my boys.

Kids with dreadlocks, who barely shaved, kids with acne.

There were no seats left. There were no seats anywhere. People had brought chairs in from the hall and were sitting in the back and side aisles.

Father Bill put on a white robe over his civilian clothes, zipped it up, then the music stopped. People talked loud for a minute or two, then grew quiet.

Father Bill was tall, had thinning hair, and looked at least ten years younger than his age.

"Good morning, everybody," he said.

"Good morning, Father Bill," everyone in the room said.

"Father Bill, grateful and recovering alcoholic and addict and powerless over—" he paused.

"A lot of things."

He said that it was Memorial Day weekend, and that Memorial Day had been first observed in 1869 to remember the fallen Union soldiers of the American Civil War.

The holiday had since expanded to help us memorialize, to remember, our dead. And because here at Caron we deal with a deadly, killing disease, and because so many of us have lost friends and loved ones to this disease, he said he'd like to begin by having us call out, and in that way remember, the names of our dead.

"So please," he said, "just call out the names of your fallen ones."

There was absolute silence for maybe a minute. I could feel my skin rise. I could feel it move.

"Carlos," someone said. A young woman down near the front said.

Robin.

Bobby...Jimmy.

Wendy.

John.

Then there was a stream, a river, a sea, an ocean, of names.

Merrill.

Donna.

Carmen.

Greer.

Ivan.

Trent.

Mary.

"Liza," Levon said.

"Ruthie," a big woman said, then started sobbing and gulping air.

All over the room, people were crying. There were wet eyes and faces everywhere.

Carol, Carley, Kim, Junie, Ed, Ryan, Dad, Tony, Brett, Aunt Jean, Cassie, Martha, Paul, Gramma.

Some people in some rows were hanging on to each other, and swaying as though in the same wind.

Dennis.

Lisa.

Ellen.

Jason.

Jessica.

Alison.

Jevon.

Kirsten.

Karen.

Stewart.

"Lauren," I suddenly called out.

She was twenty years old, all those years ago, and she had dark hair and green eyes. She took pain pills and diet pills, and she went from Newton High School to the Massachusetts College of Art, and she painted big lush oil canvasses that looked like Monet on drugs.

Like Lauren on drugs.

She hated her mom, adored her dad, and she stayed up for days and nights and days, smoking cigarettes, drinking coffee, reading books, painting, mixing pain pills with diet pills, not eating.

We talked on the phone and she said that she wanted to go to a Greek island and walk around naked, and then she wanted to never leave her dorm room, and she thought Poe was a genius.

She asked me if I knew that Poe had died in a gutter, dead drunk, in the rain, on Election Day in Baltimore.

Isn't that cool? she said.

Rick.

Denny.

Earl.

Lucy.

Brandy.

Three rows down, Marcel shouted, "Pia."

Norton.

John.

Pete.

Peter.

Levon said, "Zared."

"Donny, Chris, Doug," I called.

Donny had lunatic blue eyes, was a berserk street-fighter, Chris was gentle, scary-smart, and Doug was six-four or -five and dressed up in black tights, a black doublet. He was Hamlet, with a bottle of bourbon in one fist.

And the names kept coming, and I found myself crying, and I didn't even know why. Because of Lauren and Donny, Chris and Doug?

Because of the kids down front?

Because everyone who died took a piece of us with them?

Father Bill was up front. Nodding now and then. His face long. His face sad.

And I didn't know what was happening or why it was happening. Standing there in a fucking Catholic Mass with my half-Jewish, junkie friend, sobbing, perhaps for all these lost departed people. Sobbing because I hadn't slept more than two or three hours a night in more than ten days. Sobbing because I was withdrawing from benzos, was down to one milligram at bedtime, and I was so raw I felt like I had been skinned.

Felt like I could cry at sunlight, wind, trees, a smile, laughter, a speck of dirt, a fly.

It was so fucked-up.

I was so fucked-up.

I had not cried in years. I was an Irish-Catholic guy. I did not cry.

Then an envelope from Liam arrived Monday afternoon.

Len the C.A. gave it to me in the lounge, and the rule was that you had to open mail in front of a staff person in case someone tried to send you drugs.

I saw "Liam Cody," in pencil, in the upper left corner of the envelope, and I started to shake. With happiness, love, fear? There was so much.

"Steady, pal," Len said. He had a goatee, he smiled.

"My son," I said.

He put his hand on my shoulder. "Go read it in your room."

I was almost crying already. This was getting crazy, this withdrawal.

I sat on the bed, feet up, my back to the wall. The window was open, and there was a small breeze coming in. Every minute or so, a car went by on the road several hundred yards away.

The letter was written in pencil, on college-lined notebook paper, with the three binder holes on the left.

"Dear Dad," it began. "So lately I've been reading *The Things They Carried* and listening to Tom Waits. I realized these are two of my favorite things.

"I get so frustrated when I try to explain them to other people.

"I miss you. I miss how you get me. I got you and you got me. We could sit for hours and discuss any topic. If someone tape-recorded our conversations I swear we'd be the most sought-after genius' in the world.

"Sometimes, no a lot of the time, when I'm in school I say something and I feel like no one gets it. That's when I question myself. I wonder sometimes am I insane or just a fucking genius.

"That's probably a really extreme way of putting it.

"Anyways, I seriously miss you and especially our talks. Towards the end (before you left) I was starting to get angry with you. I felt like we never talked. Maybe because we didn't.

"Those talks were where I felt smart and where my grades didn't matter. I guess I started to resent the fact that every time I went to get emotional support my source was too tired or too fucked up to help. I went as far as to say sometimes it feels like we only live in a one-parent household."

I paused, bumped my head several times against the wall behind me. I lifted the blind on the window, saw two women walking on a path at the bottom of the long broad lawn.

There were trees, there was sky.

Liam wrote, "I hate the idea of it. That's why we need you back, healthy. So there's no more resentment, no more hiding, and no more loneliness.

"That doesn't mean rush it, or come back too soon. I trust the docs know how long you need to be there. I know it sucks being there, but if you think about it this way maybe it'll help: they're making it so you can watch us grow up. So you can come to our college graduations, our weddings, so you can see our children and get called a grandpa.

"So when you see these things, they aren't blurry, drug-infused memories, they're as clear in your head as the photos taken to capture the memory. So when you look at a photo you can provide the smells and the sounds and you can be satisfied that even when you tripped up and fell down again in your life you climbed out of every hole, gave the Grim Reaper the finger, and saw your children prove to you that it was worth fighting alcoholism and depression.

"If you do your job and get healthy, I promise we'll do ours and make you proud the best we can.

"Love, Liam."

He didn't seem to want to be born, though he tried and tried. He seemed to have had a fiery ambivalence. Because labor began on a gray April Sunday, went on the whole day, and we were in the hospital by late afternoon.

It went on and on and on. The contractions, the astonishment of pain, and Liz not crying, not screaming, but wincing, gray-faced, grim as a widow.

And the doctor finally saying at five or six on Monday morning that this was back labor, and they'd have to do a C-section.

An hour later, in the operating room, the surgeon held up this bloody, purple red-headed thing, said, "Looks like we got a linebacker here," and Lowell the anesthesiologist said, "Watch him pink up," and he did.

He weighed nine pounds, was twenty and one half inches long, and was born at seven a.m.

His first word, I remembered again, was juice, and after putting a cloth on his teddy bear a few months later, his first sentence was, Bear sleep.

He cried, he cooed, he burbled, he blew circles of sound in the air.

His first best friend was Maddy. Early on, they had a fight over a small truck in the sandbox at Maddy's house. When Liam got firm control of the truck, he hit Maddy over the head with it.

But rather than ruining their friendship, it seemed to seal something in their shared ferocity. They were hard to part for more than a half dozen years.

So Liam and I got each other, so often, on the third floor. In my office. And it was a floor, and room, that had been transformed.

There were things in the old attic from previous owners and occupants. There was an entire box of twenty-four coffee cups, with information and a phone number for a mortgage company on the side. There were several boxes of dishes and saucer—with a delicate blue line around the rim of each. There was a heavy wooden wardrobe, covered with many coats of varnish. Inside were rolled window shades leaning against a corner.

There was life-size, oblong box made of thin plywood, with a hinged cover, that looked like a poor man's coffin. There was nothing inside.

Don was our carpenter, and we had known him as long as we had owned the house. He was tall and lean, quiet, had very long hair in a ponytail, and had lived in Maine. Austin had once seen Don, with ponytail, working with a chainsaw, and said, Qui-Gon Jinn, referring to the Liam Neeson Jedi knight in *Star Wars*.

Room by room, window by window, Don was ripping, smash-ing, hammering and sanding our house from a beater into a sweet little place. He was doing it over the course of years, but it was happening.

And the attic was one of those impossible jobs. It was just so damned ugly, so depressing, so way past redemption.

The first thing Don did was rip out the vent, and cut a huge hole in the west wall. Then he took the coffin and tossed it out the hole, into October sunshine. He broke up the wardrobe, sent it out the hole, and then piece by piece, part by part, he ripped and hacked with a crowbar, and threw things toward the crunchy leaves of the tree out front.

Don brought in roll after roll of pink insulation in tan sheeting, thin boards of silver insulation, and at least fifteen or twenty pieces of sheetrock.

After a week, the attic was no longer the attic. It was light and bright, it was sheetrock and fresh wood, and new plywood for the floor. He cut two holes in the north roof for skylights.

When the skylights were in place, when the three windows overlooking the maple and the street out front were done, when there were pine baseboards, a sturdy railing around the stairway, Don went to work on the bookcases.

They ran on the east and west sides of the room, and they were eleven inches deep so that I could double-stack books. The shelves were pine and had narrow posts every five feet.

By the end, the beautiful room was white, was brimming with light, and everything that was not white was bare wood. It was my office, a room I had dreamed about for a long time.

Besides my workspace, there was a green leather shrink's chair with footstool, a captain's chair, and in one corner, a futon with wool blankets and pillows for reading and naps.

Up there I could read, listen to music, write novels, talk on the phone. I could correct student papers, visit with friends, do email.

I could stare out the window.

I could avoid Liam, avoid Austin, avoid Liz.

I could take drugs, more and more and more drugs, and nobody would know. In the beautiful room, on the futon with the wool blanket, I could put a plastic trash bag over my head, cinch it.

14

C hit Chat was almost filled, as though somebody knew something in advance. Because this was a Wednesday night, and the crowds were never that big for a regular AA speaker meeting.

But the Young Men and Women's Adolescent Units were there, Relapse, Men and Women's Primary, and Extended Care from across the big road were there as well. Plus there were lots of staff, and stray anonymous people too.

The lights went off and on, off and on, same as at the theater, then people read the Preamble, the Steps, How It Works, the Traditions.

"Please welcome Tommy," the woman at the podium said.

A short guy, maybe fifty, walked up from the front row. He wore tan dress pants with pleats, and black loafers so polished they shot reflected light that hurt your eyes. His blue oxford shirt was starched, and he was bald, had very pale skin, and looked sick.

"That's Tommie I.E., not Tommy Y.," he said.

"And I am an alcoholic, and I am an addict."

His voice was deep and gravelly, not a voice I would have expected from a short, sick guy.

"How're you all doing?" he said.

People called: "Good."

"Great."

"Shitty."

"Okay."

"Shaky."

"Puking."

Tommie smiled. He nodded. He looked over the room, side to side, up and down.

"I hear you," he said. "I hear you. I really do."

"About a year and a half ago, I was sitting right over there," and he pointed to where those of us in Men's Primary were sitting.

"I was wearing one of those red bracelets on my wrist, and I was good, I was shitty, I was okay, I was shaking, and I was puking."

He nodded and smiled some more. He looked up and down and side to side.

"Eighteen months ago. Swear to God.

"And along with good and shitty, there were so many other things too. Things like pissed-off, resentful, ashamed, stupid and smart, and scared. Really fucking scared. And really fucking confused.

"Like, How did I wake up in this nightmare? How did I get here? Where exactly did I take the wrong turn?"

Tommie looked us over some more. He had dark eyes, and they seemed to take us in.

"Am I making sense?" he asked. "You have any idea what I'm talking about?

"Cause none of this was supposed to happen. Not to me. This was the kind of shit that happened to other people. People who had bad luck. People who made bad decisions, or who had bad parents, people who were mean and vicious and somehow deserved this.

"Not people—definitely not people—like you and me.

"I mean—I mean—what I'm trying to tell you is that my dad was this prominent Philadelphia lawyer. He planned estates for people with a lot of money. And he had this big office that was all wood and leather and it had all those leather-bound law books covering a wall of his office. And my mom shopped and hosted parties and looked gorgeous all the time, and they had me and my sister.

"We had this big brick house, we had a live-in maid, we had cars, a house on the shore, and—Jesus."

Tommie stepped back and to the side of the podium.

"This sounds kind of disgusting," he said. "Pretty smug and self-satisfied, right?"

Someone in the back, a young woman, said, "Yeah."

Tommie laughed.

"You're right, honey," he said. "It was."

He put a hand on the back of his neck. He nodded slowly, smiled slowly.

"Lemme pause, lemme make a little detour down a side road, and tell you a story within a story, to mix metaphors, then I'll get back to the main road.

"That be okay?"

Jake said, "Sure," smiling under that big head of hair.

"It's a real honor to be here, up front, behind this podium, talking to you. To be standing here and not sitting there."

Everyone laughed.

"Cause I used to sit there feeling miserable and think, Could I ever be clean and sober and stand up there and talk? It was a dream, baby.

"And now I come every few months, and it's such an important commitment to me. You people keep me sober.

"So the drive from Philadelphia, where I live and work, is a little over an hour. I'm a physician, and that's part of my problem in thinking I'm smarter than I actually am.

"You all know the Doctor God thing? Doctors are supposed to know everything, they make obscene amounts of money, they make decisions about matters of life and death, and people, many many people, think they walk on water.

"I know that the mothers of most doctors think their sons are God. Or holier than thou. At the very least, they walk on water."

Tommie smiled big and wide. Tommie was having a good time.

One seat over, Bert was watching him, looking puzzled. Alan was in front of me sitting straight as a soldier, and Arnold was next to him, his head on his chest.

Outside the windows, all the trees and bushes were in leaf and bloom, the big sloping lawn was dense and green and shadowed, and just past the white slatted fences, a car with yellow headlights like eyes would flash by every few minutes.

"Right before I left Philly, before I got on the road for here, I stopped in at the I.C.U. unit at the hospital to check on my patients. Because they're the ones who are in critical shape, they're the ones who need the most attention, and it's always sobering—yeah, sobering—to go there.

"Because those people are in really really tough shape. They're right at the edge of death, every one of them.

"When you go into Intensive Care it's like a spaceship. It honest-to-God is. Just glass and more glass, and that real shiny metal, and all those machines with jagged lines and dots and hums and bings and blips. And half the people are wearing masks and pale blue uniforms.

"And the patients in the beds. My God. The patients in their beds."

He had a sad look on his face. He looked down. He shook his head slowly.

"I mean, you've all seen an I.C.U. unit, you know what it looks like. Some of you have been on Intensive Care, if you remember at all."

"Oh yeah," Max said.

Half the people in the hall turned around. Max was standing in the back of the auditorium, his long face grim.

Tommie pointed to him.

"He knows," Tommie said. "He knows.

"How long were you there?" Tommie asked.

"I don't know," Max said.

There was laughter.

Tommie rocked on his heels. He rocked on the balls of his feet.

"The patients lie there, and you might see their fingers and toes move slightly, you might see their eyelids flutter or their mouths move a bit, but mostly you check the machines for signs of life. For heartbeat and respiration.

"And the tubes run into them in just about every orifice. Into the urethra, the nose, mouth, the arms, back of the hands, the legs, you name it.

"And you know what? They need every damn one of them to stay alive. Those tubes take away waste, and they bring medicine, oxygen, fluids, nutrition, everything to sustain life.

"And there's a phrase on I.C.U. This commonly used phrase. The doctors say it began with the nurses, and the nurses say it began with the doctors, of course, because it's kind of a brutal phrase.

"It's not kind of, it is a brutal phrase.

"Circling the drain.

"Ever heard that?

"That's what we say about patients who are on I.C.U. That they're circling the drain. And they're about to go down. They're about to die.

"And there's so much truth to that, brutal as it is, brutal as it sounds. The patients are going around and around and around and around. And they get closer to the drain each time they go around.

"Our job, the job of the doctors and nurses, is to push them back from the drain, to keep them as far away as we possibly can. Because the natural tendency here, the pull of nature and gravity, is toward the drain.

"And if we can keep them safely away, for a few minutes, for hours, for a day or two or three, they might rally, they might find the strength of body and spirit to fight back. To be able to do for themselves what those tubes have been doing. To make it out of the I.C.U."

He paused and looked us over.

Outside, the sky in the east was dark, and the big lawn was all shadow.

"Each of those people, just about every one, has a terminal disease. And each one is a patient. And guess why I'm telling all of you about them?

"Not just that I stopped in to check on them before coming here, or because I was thinking about them on the drive over to Caron.

"Notice what I called them?

"Notice what I said each of them suffered from?"

Chit Chat was unusually silent.

Nobody laughed, coughed, whispered to anybody else.

Tommie stood quietly behind the podium for what seemed like a very long time. Not one of us moved.

"Those people on Intensive Care are patients. And guess what they have on their wrists, usually their right wrists?"

People were looking down at their wrists.

I didn't look down although I wanted to, but I could feel the loose bracelet resting on the back of my hand.

"Right," Tommie said. "One of those I.D. bracelets with your name and any drug allergies written on it.

"And guess what you people are, here at Caron? Here at the Caron Treatment Center?"

He looked us over, and I swear, for a moment, his eyes rested on me.

"You people are patients."

He paused.

"Just like the patients on Intensive Care."

He stood quietly for a full minute. Tommie knew how to use the long pause.

"And guess what else?"

He nodded. He did not smile.

"Like so many of the people on I.C.U. who have terminal illnesses, every single one of us in this room"—and here he lifted his hand and moved it slowly, sweeping the entire room—"every last breathing soul in here has a terminal illness, including me."

He lowered his voice to a near-whisper.

"It's called alcoholism and drug addiction."

He paused, and he paused longer. A full minute. Two minutes.

"And make no mistake. No fucking, bleeding mistake. This disease will take you down hard, it will kill you. And it will do it in an astonishing variety of ways. From overdose to car wreck, suicide to cirrhosis, hep B to gangrene. It'll get you in a thousand surprising, shocking, degrading ways.

"But there's hope here. Truly, truly, truly. Real, life-saving hope. For every last one of you sitting there.

"Because that's my job. To bring hope. To try to help. And that's the mission of the staff here, even though you guys think their job is to prevent you from talking to the women, and you women think their job is to prevent you from talking to the men."

He waved his hand.

"That's just a small part of their job. "

People said, "No."

"Okay," Tommie said. "It's a medium-sized part of their job."

Everyone was laughing, chuckling, giggling. Men and women were waving and gesturing back and forth across the aisle.

"You've all heard it," Tommie said. "None of this is news to you. That addiction to drugs or alcohol is a disease. The disease concept has been around a while, it is not fresh news.

"But it somehow doesn't get through. Because one of the major features of this disease is that it tells you nearly all the time that you don't have a disease, that you're really fine, and that next time you drink or do drugs it's gonna be different.

"Now on I.C.U., when we're able to keep someone pushed back from the drain, and they rally, and we're able to remove the tubes, and they get up from bed, go to a step-down unit and eventually leave the hospital and go home, they're usually pretty shaken up by their experience. So they usually limit their salt intake, change their diet, they exercise, see their doctor, take their medicine. Not all the time, but often. There's nothing in their disease that tells them they don't have a disease.

"Do addicts do that?"

He looked us over. Tommie moved his head from side to side.

"Not very often. Not very often at all.

"And that's one of the things that's so heartbreaking about addiction. We can take the tubes out, we can get up from the bed, we can get as way the fuck far away from that drain as we possibly can, and we can do it almost any time we choose to.

"Because we're all, every one of us here, without a single exception, circling the drain. We're going around and around and around. And that drain is there. There's a grate over it, but that just covers the black hole. That just covers the darkness.

"Because that's where we're all headed, whether we know it or now, whether we like it or not.

"And in so many important ways, that's what it is to be human. We come out of a warm wet hole and we're going back to a wet hole. There's absolutely no way around those basic facts. We're born and we die. And what we do in between is called life.

"And it's called the human condition. In some huge, crucial way, to be human, to be alive, is to circle the drain. Only if you don't have a terminal illness you circle it from pretty far away. So far away, in fact, that you may not even be aware that you are circling a drain, or that the drain is there at all."

Tommie paused again. He touched the starched collar of his blue shirt.

"But when you have a terminal disease, you need to be aware that you have that disease, and that the drain is very close, and you need help pushing yourself away from the drain.

"You need help," he nearly shouted.

He stopped. He looked.

"You need help," he said more quietly.

Once more he paused.

"You need help," he whispered into the microphone.

In a normal voice he said, "I need help."

I had never heard the room so quiet. Nobody coughed or moved. Nobody seemed to breathe.

It was now full dark outside. When a car passed it was just two lights on a dark field.

"So when people say they're here to share their experience, strength and hope, they really are. They do that in AA.

They do that every minute of every day. And they don't do it because they're nice people, or because they're do-gooders. They do it for very selfish reasons.

"They need you as much as you need them.

"I need you guys, you all, you every one of you, probably as much or more than you might need me. Cause I can't stay sober without you. I really can't. I'm a drunk man, I'm a guy who puts needles in his veins and pops pills, I'm a dead man, without you.

"Just standing here and being in this room reminds me of how much time I spent in this auditorium. And it was a very powerful time for me. Powerful awful and powerful good. Despair and hope.

"Let's face it, detox is rough. Detox is very very rough.

"Father Bill likes to say that if you can't remember your last detox, you haven't had it yet.

"I can remember mine. The shaking, the tremors, the sweats, the insomnia, and the terrible feeling of panic all the time. Skin-crawling, heart-racing panic—all the time. God.

"But I heard over and over that I could make this the last detox, the last feeling of utter misery. They said to me, You don't ever have to drink or drug again.

"I'd heard that one before. But I don't think I'd ever heard it either.

"You know how you hear something, but you don't. Or you see something, but not really. Or you understand something, except you don't.

"Well maybe because my defenses were so shattered, I was more open to things. Maybe I started to hear and see and understand in a slightly new way.

"I don't know. But somehow grew out of the misery. Something flew up out of the ashes.

"That's what I wish for you people. That's what I pray for each of you. That something slightly new begins to happen for you here."

Tommie paused again. He looked at the ceiling and the high walls. It was deep dark outside now. The lights were on in here, and it was though we were an island of light in the sea of dark. All these drunks and addicts were huddled together on the island.

"I didn't want to come here and tell you all about my disasters when I drank and used drugs. All the tragedy, the smash-ups, the lies, broken promises, lost jobs, arrests, busted marriages, the cheating, stealing, DUI's, the monster hangovers, hospital stays, jail time, the long sorry litany of an alcoholic's life.

"You hear that so often.

"I think when people go to speak and they hear that they're supposed to share their experience, strength and hope, they fix on experience, and they assume that means only their experience of being degraded by the disease.

"But they tell the story out of their own deep need.

"Still, what about their experience of recovery? Their experience of hope and strength? Their experience of AA? Of life without alcohol and drugs?

"That's what I wanted to try to bring to you tonight. A little bit more of that, and perhaps a little bit less of the tragic memories. Because we all have the tragic memories, the sordid experiences, the really cruel things that this disease did not only to each of us but to those around us, to those who love us."

Tommie shot his cuff, checked his watch, and said, "We still have time, and I mean that in more ways than one.

"We still have time," he said again.

He walked to one side of the podium, then to the other side. He looked into the audience, squinted, waved to someone.

Then he was behind the podium again. He took a deep breath.

"Okay, gang. A few more things, then I'll release you to this gorgeous spring night."

He looked at us some more, smiled wide.

"Deal?"

"Deal," half the room said.

"Okay," he said.

"I'm a surgeon. I'm one of those Type A personalities. I don't like to screw around. I like to get in there and do something."

He held his hand out, spread his fingers.

"See that steady hand," he said. "Absolutely sure and steady.

"Remember the old saying, A surgeon cuts someone not to harm but to heal.

"But there's always been a part of me that wasn't a surgeon type. That was more reflective, more measured, more circumspect.

"I like movies and the theater and art. I go to museums, and believe me you do not run into many surgeons at the museum. You see them at football games and drag races, at the stock exchange and bars.

"And another big thing for me is books—history and biography and especially poetry and novels. I totally love novels. And you just don't find surgeons reading novels unless it's an action novel, or a murder, madness, mayhem novel. Car chases, guns, sex and such.

"Now you may be wondering what this has to do with addiction and recovery, but please bear with me. I'll loop back there on this crooked, winding path. I'll find a way to bring us safely home.

"The thing about a good novel, and I don't mean bodice rippers, and action novels, and murder, madness and mayhem novels, is that they take you in to a dream, they take you in to the world of the writer.

"They bring news from that person's deepest places to our deepest places. The places that are full of loss and grief, love, longing, hope and fear, and the deepest things that are in us.

"What they do is connect us. They let us know that we're not alone, even though, so much of the time, we think and feel that we are alone.

"Because what does addiction do to us? What does drinking and drugs do to us?

"Does it bring us love?"

Another look, side to side, over the audience.

"Does it connect us to one another?"

Tommie paused still again.

"You find a lot of human love in a crack house? You get that authentic human connection in a bar?

"How about this? You get nurtured and you find that deep caring from your dealer?

"Is that what you're looking for?

"Because I was," he said. "I really was."

He nodded.

"I took that shot of morphine, of oxy, and I was looking for warmth, for that melting away feeling, for that oceanic sense that everyone and everything was one.

"You know how long it lasted?

"In the beginning it lasted an hour or two. Then a half hour. Then five minutes. Then I couldn't find it at all.

"And novels and stories, they're the real thing. The real connection. They're as old as people sitting around campfires.

"You come in from work, you say to your daughter, How was your day? She tells you a story. It's what makes us human.

"A wonderful writer, Joan Didion, said, We tell ourselves stories in order to live.

"In order to live," he whispered.

"It's no small thing. It's like I.C.U., my friends. These are matters of life and death.

"You don't tell your story, you don't listen to other people's stories, then you're in big trouble. You're so close to the drain there may be no help for you.

"And that's what happens in AA. People tell their stories. They connect. They learn what it is to be human.

"Every meeting, every phone call, every encounter before and after meetings, is a small and large act of storytelling.

"It's scary shit too. Especially if you've been encased in booze and drugs for years and years.

"But it's cool.

"You'll live."

n12

L iz had light brown hair that, in summer, grew even lighter, and became almost blond.

She was five foot three and a half inches tall, and weighed about one hundred and fifteen pounds.

She grew up in a small city in east Tennessee, near the foothills of the Smoky Mountains.

She went to church camp.

Her dad owned several shoe stores, was on the board of the local bank, an elder of the Presbyterian Church, and a longtime member of the Rotary Club.

Her mom was from Georgia and had been a schoolteacher, and moved to Knoxville to work for the Tennessee Valley Authority.

Liz worked in the summer as a lifeguard at a pool. She worked in one of her dad's shoe stores.

She read often and deeply.

She graduated first in her high school class.

She went to Davidson in North Carolina, one of the finest small colleges in the country, a school that produced more Rhodes

Scholars per capita than any college nationwide. She graduated Phi Beta Kappa.

She learned Swahili, and spent a year teaching in a rural school for girls in Kenya. The colors in Kenya were vivid and deep. The sky was cerulean blue, the earth copper, the skin of many people was so black it was almost blue.

She went to New York City and worked in publishing. She knew very few people in the city, and on weekends she went to the Natural History Museum, to the Met, and when she overheard conversations she would imagine herself in those lives, she would dream herself into other worlds. She yearned for Monday, when she would be back at work, and she could talk to and be around other people.

After three years in New York, she moved to Durham, worked part-time at Duke, and spent much of her time working on poetry.

She was awarded a fellowship to study in the Master of Fine Arts program in poetry at Cornell University. She was the admissions committee's top pick.

She moved to Ithaca, in upstate New York, in August 1985. She was twenty-eight years old.

I left Medfield State Hospital after thirty days. I was clean and sober and very scared.

I weighed one hundred thirty-two pounds when I arrived at Medfield, and weighed close to one-forty when I left.

I was six foot one and a half inches tall. I had dark brown hair and blue eyes.

I was twenty-two years old, the age when many people graduate from college.

So I didn't drink or use drugs any more, not for a long long time. I went to college at the University of Massachusetts at Boston. I rode Red Line trains to Columbia Station in the Dorchester section of Boston, and there, on the same spit of land with the university, was the cluster of twenty-story buildings, the Columbia Point housing projects, now half boarded up.

I rode the trains, read books, wrote papers, and became an English major. I got A's in most classes.

After four years I graduated With Distinction in English and Senior Honors in Creative Writing.

For three years I worked with deaf-blind, developmentally disabled teenagers at the Perkins School for the Blind in Watertown, just outside Boston.

In February of my third year at Perkins, I got a call from Cornell University, saying that I had been accepted into their Master of Fine Arts program in fiction writing. They would give me a tuition waiver and a stipend to live on.

Liz and I met for the first time in August 1985, at a party given by the novelist Alison Lurie for the MFA students. We were standing on the back deck at Alison's house, and Liz and I found ourselves next to each other, and began talking slowly and awkwardly.

There was a hay field in the distance, golden in the late-summer sunlight.

"Where are you from?"

"Tennessee. You?"

"Boston."

"Where'd you go to school?"

"Davidson. You?"

"U. Mass. Boston."

We looked at each other's shoes, shirt collars, at ears, hair, anywhere but at eyes.

"You like it here?" I finally asked.

"Sure. After seven days. You?"

"Yeah."

"Where you living?" I asked.

"South Hill."

Long pause. Real long pause.

"How about you?" she asked.

She had fair skin, faint freckles. She was pretty in a quiet kind of way.

How about me what? I thought.

"Where you living?" she asked.

"Oh," I said, and looked at my shoes. Brown chukkas with leather laces. Then looked at her shoes. Tan sandals.

"So where you living?" she asked.

"Oh, sorry. Collegetown."

She blushed. I think I blushed too. It felt that way.

I said something about Davidson College, that they had had good basketball teams not too long ago.

She looked puzzled. Everything we said to each other seemed to evoke puzzlement.

"Small, good college. Went pretty far in the NCAA's."

"The who?"

"National Collegiate Athletic Association tournament."

She looked a little less puzzled.

"It's a national college basketball tournament. March Madness. National television. Usually the big basketball powers—Kansas, UCLA, Kentucky, North Carolina—are there and go deep in the elimination process. It was unusual and sweet that a place like Davidson would do so well against the big places."

"I know," she said evenly.

What an ice queen, I thought.

"I was trying to say something nice about your school."

She moved her head slowly from side to side.

She said, "No need to."

Then there was nothing to say.

Over the next few months I saw her on campus, in the halls of Goldwin Smith, the building that housed the English Department, and on the streets of Collegetown. She always had her head down, and she was always alone.

Partly to be a pain in the ass, partly to jump into her consciousness, I said hello to her every time. She'd look up, startled, take a second to recognize who I was, and mouth the word, "Hi."

Then I started to think that she was shy, she was lonely, she was stuck up here with all the fast-talking, aggressive Northerners, and maybe I should just leave her be. Not that I thought of her that much anyway.

I lived in a basement apartment in a house on the side of a steep hill. There was a small bedroom and living room, a tiny kitchen, and a bathroom that would make an airplane bathroom seem capacious. It had a rusting tin shower, from which you could reach and turn the stove on.

There were pipes in the ceiling, and beyond the bedroom wall was the furnace, which rumbled off and on from October until April. When people came into the hall on the first floor, they'd stamp the snow off their shoes directly over my bed.

Most of the time I read books, wrote short stories, went to classes, took long solitary walks around the Cornell campus, and went to movies almost every night on campus.

Ithaca is built on three hills that are set at the southern end of Cayuga Lake. The lake is forty miles long, a mile or more wide in many places, and hundreds of feet deep.

Cornell is on East Hill, and is bounded by very deep gorges that look like something from South America. Many of its buildings are made of heavy gray sandstone, and its quads are broad and lined with giant trees.

From the front steps of Goldwin Smith Hall, you could look across the quad, past bronze statues, between stately buildings, and on hills far off you could see silos and farms, and thin roads, and patches of fields, brown and green, and if you looked closely and carefully you could see tractors moving in the fields.

I had never lived or worked anywhere so beautiful. At U. Mass. Boston one of the principal associations was with the crash and screech of trains on the Red Line, and with gigantic gas tanks on the Southeast Expressway, the main artery into Boston.

Cornell was heaven.

And the university was paying for everything. All I had to do was read and write, show up for classes, do the work.

If I was lonely, so what. I'd meet people eventually.

By the spring, I had met people, was beginning to hang out, and life was awfully good. I still saw Liz here and there, said hello once in a while, and she even said hello to me once when I wasn't looking.

Then we were assigned to summer teaching; very small groups of two or three were apprenticed to an experienced instructor to teach a summer class. Liz and I were in the same small group. We'd be around each other every day.

And she wasn't an ice queen, or a stiff, or a snob, or a bitch.

She was kind of shy and quiet.

She was pretty funny in this shy and quiet way.

She received a poem from a student that began, "A plane crash,/What a fiery hell,/Two hundred bodies make an awful smell."

The poem went on for ten stanzas, a rhyme and a catastrophe in each.

She was really smart.

Ithaca and Cornell were amazing in summer.

The water did not freeze in the gorges but gurgled. The wind did not howl, it whispered. The trees and bushes were a riot of leaves and flowers, and most of the undergraduates were gone.

I called her one evening to see if she wanted to see a movie.

"What movie?" she asked.

Did it matter? I thought.

Ice queen.

"An American In Paris."

"Okay," she said.

Not wildly enthusiastic, but it was better than staying home alone.

But she seemed friendly enough, and she looked very pretty in this shy and quiet way, and I had only seen the movie on television, never on a big screen, and it was good, really good.

I walked her home, careful to not touch or even brush against her, under the leafy trees, the fragrant flower beds, the lighted windows of houses.

Then she did a startling thing, after we had not spoken for a minute or two. She took my hand.

She took my hand.

What was with that?

Was that a Southern thing? A Protestant thing?

Like, What's playing?

Like, No need to?

The better part of a year spent barely saying hello, probably not remembering my name.

Now we were walking home and she took my hand.

Then maybe a block or two later, a particularly dark part of the street because of trees or a broken streetlight or both, she said, "Wait."

Put her hand on my arm, went up on her toes, leaned, kissed me lightly on the lips.

Soft, of course.

Deft.

Was that a Southern thing?

She wrote:
Some days just happen, the way
blank stalks flare into lilies;
but most I wait for.

I wrote:
He disappeared on a Friday afternoon in October. He was nine or ten years old, and he may have been riding a bicycle, or he may have been walking. The day was warm, and he was probably alone—somewhere in Newton, outside Boston.

She lived in a house with three other women, all of whom were Cornell graduate students. The house was a half block from a foot bridge that crossed a gorge at Six Mile Creek.

She wrote:
At the edge of a cloud's mammoth
shadow I admire its indifference
to the rushed ground. So clear a marker—
but it sweeps on too fast to follow,
or disintegrates into sameness.
I look for scarce borders,

and love especially a sunny rain.

I told her about my alcoholism and drug addiction, that between the ages of fourteen or fifteen until I was twenty-three, I
was a pretty messed-up individual, that I had finally been commit-
ted to a state hospital in Massachusetts. That I had been clean and
sober ever since.

"And that's how long ago?" she asked.

"Just about a decade," I said.

I wrote:

He was wearing jeans and a baseball cap and sneakers, and
maybe he was on Walnut Street, near Newtonville Square, and a
car pulled up. A blue car, a red car, a car with out-of-state plates,
and the driver rolled down the window, and said, Hey, said, Hello,
asked for directions, wanted to know the time.

She didn't flinch, she didn't blink, she didn't swallow. She didn't
say, Holy cow! You've got to be kidding! Or, Oh my God!

She said, "Good for you."

She said, "Thanks for telling me."

She asked, "Does it matter that I've never done drugs, ever?
That I might have been tipsy a few times in my life?"

I said I didn't think so. I guess I didn't know.

She wrote:

Only clouds. Not old people
or children, not the city's ferment
of squalor and glamour—I distill
the body in cloud-curves, neon
in sunrise, breathing crowds in

a billion wisps of vapor.

I wrote:
You want a lift? the driver may have asked, and Ford stopped, turned, smiled. He had freckles, straight brown hair, blue eyes.

Sometimes we walked for hours on the trails that snaked all over the Cornell campus. They wound for miles in and around small and large gorges, on paths through woods, around lakes and ponds and waterfalls. We walked across quads where the windows in most buildings were dark.

The later it grew, the quieter the campus became, and the more pronounced the sound of wind and water flowing in streams and gorges.

The moon rose higher and higher, and cast shadows, and even though both of us had been awake since early in the morning, neither of us felt the least bit tired.

We were floating on something—night air, moonlight, the scent of flowers on the late July night.

She wrote:
I sat on an island,
level with the level sea, and watched
the clouds form and re-form their
cold allegiances. Piles of them
neared, ebbed, withdrew,
while the blunt sun took cover,
or leaked a hazy glare.

She looked at me in the shadow of moonlight, in woods that circled a small lake, at close to two in the morning. She put her hand on my wrist.

"I need to ask you something," she said.

I looked at her, and the world shadowed her face.

I nodded.

"When you were using drugs," she said, "when you were drinking. Did you—?"

She put her hand to her face.

I watched her as though my life could end.

"Did you ever hurt anybody? Were you ever violent?"

I shook my head.

"Were you ever in jail?"

She was staring at me evenly.

I wrote:

This was a long time ago, and he might be someplace now, might be in some town or city, some state or country or continent. He'd be older, and he could have a new family, a family of his own, or maybe just a room to himself.

I told her about the mesh windows, the patients in slippers and pajamas, the long white halls. There were cracked plaster ceilings, and the television set in the dayroom was bolted to a heavy oak table.

Nearly all the patient bedrooms were locked during the days. So some patients slept in chairs in the dayroom.

Some wore hats—baseball hats, a Greek fisherman's cap, a Tam. One woman wore a golfing hat that had a tiny golf ball and clubs above the brim.

The staff carried rings of keys that jangled when they walked.

I wrote:

Or he might be dead. Probably he's dead. He could have drowned, could have been shot or strangled or stabbed or smothered, and left somewhere. In woods, in a dumpster, at the edge of a lake. Maybe his body was found in the Utah desert, or in a motel room, off an interstate, in Missouri or Nevada or Florida. There were blinking neon lights, anemic palm trees, the whine of traffic in the distance. An insect ticking against a window.

She asked, "How old were you?"

"Twenty-two, twenty-three."

We had begun walking again.

"But you weren't locked up?"

"Not in jail. But the hospital was a locked ward."

"You were there a month?"

"Yes. Thirty days."

The surface of Beebe Lake was smooth and flawless. The moon sat in the middle of the lake, and there was a trail of pale light that led from the moon to the far shore.

"And you were forced to go there?"

She wrote:

I practice a shined-up waiting—
tedium raised to an aerialist's
art. You in the white bed,
me on the dust-gray loveseat
in the lobby, we're dull as an aging
high-wire team, too long balanced.
We don't think of danger, but
the boring wire, increments of inches.

"Oh, yeah. I hit an intern. Got put in a straightjacket, taken to a state hospital."

"The intern," she said. "Where was he?"

"At a local hospital, outside Boston."

"Was he hurt?"

"No. It wasn't much of a punch."

The trees were tall and old, and the leaves shivered.

Every now and then I would think, This is a long way from Boston, this is a long way from Tennessee. Being on drugs was like getting abducted.

She wrote:
I sat, I wandered, ate and napped,
after my dull necessities like
a microbe under a microscope's eye.
But the eye was mine. And finally
the high mists resolved to order,
met fields of pure light, caught
fire in still after still:
The best life is change.

"And then a straightjacket?"

"Yeah."

"And that's like?"

"Like a canvas coat, with no opening at the bottom of the sleeves, just straps, so they can cross your arms in front of you, strap them down. So you can't hit anyone."

She nodded. We had stopped on the path.

She put her hand on my arm, then on the side of my face.

"God," she said. "Oh my God."

"It happens."

I looked down. I looked at our shoes.

"You do drugs, you drink, this kind of thing happens."

"And they just took you to the state ... to the state ... place?"

"Hospital. Yes."

"Just like that?"

"They get what they call a pink paper. "

"Pink paper?"

"A court order signed by a judge."

"Wow."

"Committing you to a state hospital for thirty days."

"No hearing? No lawyer? No due process?"

"No, no."

"But—"

"You're a crazy person."

She wrote:

The elevator opens on a two-part world.

the ones in white have faces like

business suits of grief. The rest—

their naked faces rock, rock

on waves of drugged muscles.

Then we were on the Arts Quad and it was one in the morning, and I said, "If you don't want anything to do with me, I'll understand."

She laughed, took my arm.

"What if I want more to do with you?"

The Arts Quad was the size of five or ten football fields. It was measured, elegant, stately, handsome, spacious.

At one in the morning it was empty of everything except trees and buildings, lawns and paths.

"You serious?" I asked.

She took my arm.

She said, "It's getting chilly.

"Let's go home," she said.

She wrote:
Things occurred to me,
and I to them. I thought
I'd better go. Any
leaf—say the reddest
fraction of that sumac—
is inexhaustible.

She had light brown hair.
She grew up in Tennessee.
She went to church camp.

16

O n day twenty-one the taper was through, and the shakes and tics, the tremors and sleeplessness, got even worse. I was sleeping an hour or two a night, at most, and Levon and Chuck were gone, and Doc was sleeping four or five hours a night, so overnights were very long and real lonely.

The Butt Hut at three a.m. was a solitary place. There was just wind and trees and darkness, and my own racing thoughts. There was just cigarette after ashy cigarette. It seemed as though I had been at Caron for half a year, and it seemed as though the time in detox, when I'd slept around the clock, had been in some other life.

Levon had gone across the street to Men's Extended Care, and that move surprised Levon and all of us who knew him. He was so bright and funny, and he was such a New York City boy; Extended Care meant an extra ninety days at Caron, with meetings and groups every day. Along with Primary it would mean one hundred twenty days in all, a third of a year at Caron.

But the statistic the staff ran by the patients and the families of patients was that only twenty percent of those who finished Primary would remain clean and sober after one year. The number for those who did the Primary and Extended Care programs was about eighty percent.

Levon came back from a meeting with his family and counselors shaken. There were no jokes, no smiles.

When I asked how he was doing, he said, "If someone told me three weeks ago that I'd even consider staying here an extra three months, I would have told them to go fuck themselves."

He said very little for several days, then he said, "Okay, he'd stay," then he was his smiling, joking self again.

Bert told him he did the right thing, Levon said, "Thanks, pal," and Marcel said he couldn't believe what he was seeing. The cats in a bag were purring.

Chuck left to get his dog, go to Atlantic City to gamble for a week, then go back to New York.

Before he went we had one last night out at the Butt Hut, this time at four a.m.

Chuck smoked Newports, I smoked Kools, and we kept giving each other cigarettes.

His sister was picking him up around nine or ten, and I said, "Can I come?"

"Any time."

Then he said, "Paul, you don't wanna come with me. Not where I'm going."

I looked at him.

"You got your shit together. You got kids, you got a life."

"You got a life too."

"Dude, I'll be doing dope. Most likely."

"No, Chuck."

"Yeah, dude, I will."

"Oh fuck, Chuck."

We laughed.

"I just love dope. That's all."

We didn't say anything for a long time. I loved dope too. Not heroin, but pills, booze.

"You're a good guy," I said. "These nights would have sucked so much worse without you."

He smiled.

"I would have been climbing the fucking trees, howling at the moon," he said. "Know what I'm saying?"

Then he flicked his lighter over and over, his face brief flashes of light dark, light dark, light dark.

After Levon and Chuck were gone, I was one of the more experienced patients, three weeks in. The Unit was filling up with new guys, guys who banged into walls when they walked, guys who seemed like they'd come in off the golf course.

Stan, my counselor, gave me the Extended Care pitch, but I said no, I had kids, a wife, a life.

He said, "You were hardly here the first week of your stay."

"Is anybody?" I asked.

"Ha ha ha," he barked.

Stan had Buddhist prayer flags that ran across the top of his window—blue, white, red, green, yellow.

He sneezed, rubbed his nose.

"Some," he said.

Then he reached for tissues, blew his nose. He got more tissues, rubbed his leaking eyes.

"The thing is, if you take away that first week, it leaves you with an extra week to go, really, to complete the thirty-one days."

An extra seven days. Seven endless days. Days were weeks. A week was a month. A week was a year.

"I've talked to Elizabeth about this," he said. "She thinks it's a pretty good idea."

"You talked to Liz?"

"Several times."

He nodded.

She was so far away I could hardly picture her.

Stan said we could arrange a conference call between Liz, me and himself and discuss the extra week.

I said, Okay, but that I doubted it.

So much of the time it seemed as though I'd never sleep until I got home to my own bed. My roommate Sam could not have been a better fit. He owned computer stores in Rhode Island, had two small kids, was married to an attorney, had been an English major at Union College. He was smart, funny, thoughtful. He was courteous.

But the idea of sleeping in a room with anyone but Liz was so strange, and being thrown in with thirty-five other guys in such close quarters, going to so many meetings and groups and lectures every day was so onerous that I longed to leave.

I wanted to see Liz, wanted to see Austin and Liam, wanted to sit in my office, lie on my bed, turn on the computer, use a phone, read a book. I wanted to drive a car, talk to a friend. I just wanted to be alone somewhere, wanted to be alone anywhere—without the press and grip of other people talking, yelling, laughing.

There were things I missed:

Real coffee. Say a double cappuccino from Gimme! on North Cayuga Street in Ithaca. One where they made a leaf design with steamed milk on the surface.

I missed my queen-sized bed.

I missed the big down comforter that was dark blue and green.

I missed how my kids would come into the room when I was reading in bed and would start to talk to me. Would tell me about a book they were reading, music they were listening to, a kid or teacher they liked or didn't like, a subject in school that excited them. How one of the assassination plots against Hitler nearly worked, except that someone in the room accidentally bumped a briefcase with a bomb in it and moved the briefcase, just how big a great white shark could grow, how Mr. Harrington was not just a great history teacher, he was the swim coach too.

I missed being alone, and absolutely clean and sober, and content and even happy, very late at night, while everyone else in the world slept, it seemed, and I read or reread a great book, a book I loved completely and utterly. *Anna Karenina* or *Ulysses* or *To the Lighthouse,* and I was with every word, every sentence, every image, allusion and metaphor.

I missed being on the front porch at my friend Doug's house, the creek just across the small road, sunlight dappling leaves, sitting in Adirondack chairs, saying everything or nothing to Doug, because in some spooky, almost uncanny way, we got each other.

And I missed Liz too. How when we were good, I was just this person she married, just this regular guy who wasn't trying to manage or control anything, just this person who accepted his humanity, his frailty.

It seemed so long since I'd felt that.

Then for the thousandth, for the ten thousandth time in the last week or two, I thought of the pain pills still sitting on the bookshelves in my office at home.

Sixty of them. Possibly sixty-five.

They weren't the benzos I would have hoped for, but they'd certainly take the edge off.

I pictured pushing a few of them through the plastic and aluminum strip, chasing down two with water, waiting twenty minutes, taking two more. And in an hour, hour and a half, I'd take six or eight or ten, and I'd begin to feel less and less pain.

A sweet, warm, liquid feeling would spread out from my torso to my legs and arms, hands, feet, fingers, toes, face, ears, and I would begin to smile and smile. Within a very short time I would feel like calling people, talking to them, being close, being kind.

The whole scene was laid out. It was more or less assured.

Get home. Make a big fuss out of being home. Pet the cats. Drink tea. Sit on the couch, or in one of the big chairs.

Then after a half hour or hour say, Gotta go check the office.

Get some time alone.

Who wouldn't want time alone after no time alone for so long?

Close the door to the third floor, go slowly up the steep stairs, turn the computer on, sit at my desk, listen carefully to make sure nobody was following me, nobody was on even the second floor.

Then when I was sure it was quiet, when I was sure I was absolutely and completely by myself, I'd go to the bookshelves in the far corner, my hands shaking, find the small plastic bag, almost not believing it was really there, then my fingers would fumble into the crinkling plastic, and I'd begin to tremble, began to shake with excitement that my luck was this good, that I could be delivered this simply and easily from the torment of withdrawal.

And I played through that scene so many times at Caron. Over and over and over. In one of the nation's finest treatment centers for addiction.

It was almost the thing that had seen me through.

I had always been a good student, when I wasn't drinking or on drugs. I never missed class, did the reading and the homework, listened.

And at Caron I'd done my best to be a good trooper. To show up on time for all the meetings and lectures, to participate, to have a good attitude, and to not piss and moan about withdrawal.

Except: I had a stash at home, and that was kind of keeping me alive. It was keeping my addiction alive.

But on day twenty-one, coming up late from dinner, I fell into step with the C.A. Kevin. He had laser blue eyes, a wonderful smile, and a general sort of AA glow.

He said, "How you doing? You getting to be short time around here."

I said, Yeah, I was, but that they were pitching me an extra week.

"That why you look like you're carrying around something?"

"Do I?"

"Well shit, Paul, don't have to be a mind reader."

I didn't say anything.

He didn't say anything.

He limped when he walked so we didn't go fast.

"How you doing?" I finally asked.

"Good," he said. "Good."

Then there was more silence.

Finally he said, "Listen, you wanna tell me something. Cause if you do, I'll listen. And you probably won't shock me."

I laughed.

"You sure of that?"

"Pretty sure."

I told him I had an office at home, and that in the corner of the office there was one last stash of pills.

"Ah," he said.

"Yeah. Is what's there."

"And that's the only stash left?"

I nodded.

"What were you figuring to do?"

"Get home, do the rest of the pills, then get on with my recovery."

Kevin laughed.

Then I started laughing.

"Pretty stupid, huh?"

"Well, it's how we think."

"Yeah."

"And you've been carrying that around?"

"Yeah."

"What do think you should do?"

"Ask my wife to get rid of them."

"Wanna use the office phone?"

"Think I'll write a letter."

He said, "Good. Thanks for telling me."

"Thank you."

Inside, I went to my room. Sam was folding laundry, putting it away.

I got a pen and pad of paper, lay on the bed, began to write.

I told Liz about the pills, and exactly where they were. I asked her to get rid of them. I said that if I ever told her I could take pills safely, pills that weren't prescribed by Adam, my doctor, that she shouldn't believe me. I was lying. It wasn't me talking. It was my addiction.

Then I tore the page from the pad, addressed and stamped an envelope.

I lay on the bed, sweating.

Sam said, "Hey."

I looked over.

"You okay?" he asked.

It was uncanny how some people just knew something was going on. First Kevin, now Sam.

So I told Sam about the pills. I asked him to read the letter.

He did. He handed it back, smiling.

"Way to go," he said.

I nodded.

"You sure you don't want to call? They'll let you use the office phone."

I laughed. "This'll get there in plenty of time."

He patted my foot, which was sticking over the side of the bed.

"C'mon," he said, "I'll walk you to the office, to the mail bag."

And it occurred to me that I might have paused. Might have set the letter on the small desk, and waited just a little. Thought about it, just a little. Kept the door open a crack.

I could easily have gone through an evening, sat through lectures, meetings, meditation, could have hung out with my brothers on D-Block, as we called ourselves, smiled, talked, listened, said the right things, nodded, shrugged, had every appearance of being appropriate, and thought of the letter sitting, unmailed.

This was classic alcoholic thinking. Absolute textbook addict reasoning.

There was a saying you heard in AA: We're as sick as our secrets.

Only my secret, which had grown and grown over the last few weeks, wasn't the secret it had been.

Kevin knew. Sam knew.

"Paul," Sam said. "Let's mail the letter."

He was reading my thoughts. People here did that. They did it all the time.

When it came to the disease, we all thought so much alike.

Sam said, "Paul. C'mon, dude." He smiled. "Let's do it. Let's get this done."

Sam had two kids. He had a terrific wife.

I got up, and we moved through the crowd in the lounge.

Kevin was sitting at the desk in the office.

"Outgoing mail, Kevin," Sam said.

Kevin looked. "Go for it," he said, then turned back to the computer on the desk.

It was a giant mail pouch on top of the small refrigerator in the corner. I opened it, checked the name, address, zip code, checked the stamp, put it in.

Sam and I went out, went to the Butt Hut, lit up. We stood on the small road.

"You feel good?" he asked.

"Yeah."

"Lighter?"

I nodded.

We smoked a little.

"Thanks," I finally said.

"It's a good thing."

After a while Sam went inside to finish his laundry. Nobody was at the Butt Hut, and I almost wanted to go back to get the letter. I almost wanted to say to Kevin and Sam that it was untrue about the pills in my office, but I was pretty sure it was true.

I was supposed to feel light and free and honest and true. But I didn't.

Maybe a little of me did. Maybe ten percent, twenty percent. Because this was cutting the cord, the lifeline, to my addiction.

But it really sucked too. Because I was shaking, I had an almost constant dread that something really bad was about to happen—my kids would get badly hurt, Liz would have a serious car wreck, I'd have a massive heart attack—and I couldn't get more than an hour or two of sleep a night.

And this could go on for months. Benzo withdrawal could go on for a year, for two years. It was a mad-ugly withdrawal.

Valium would bring immediate relief. So would Klonopin, Ativan. I would think of a dozen, of two dozen, pills that would bring instant relief.

They would cure the problem, and cause the problem.

There was always the feeling that you could count on drugs to make you feel good. The world and the people in it might frustrate you, anger you, vex you, not give you what you wanted, might make you feel lonely or unhappy or bad, but you could retreat to your office or bedroom or to your wherever, and open your bottle of pills or booze.

And you could say, Fuck you, to the frustrating, vexing world and its uncooperative people.

At least for a little while.

Brendan came out from the building. He was tall, ripped, wore a white tee-shirt and jeans. He had steel-rimmed glasses, a crew-cut, a narrow face.

Brendan was only thirty, but his hair was completely gray. He was a former Marine who had done two tours in Iraq, had been shot twice. He was a New York City transit cop. He was a huffer, a guy who did inhalants—bonding agents, cleaning solvents, spray paint.

Brendan had come in a week earlier, and despite the difference in our ages we had become almost instant brothers. Maybe it was something about being Irish.

He said, "You don't look so hot."

I nodded and shook my head.

He slapped my shoulder.

"What's up, prof?"

"Wanna walk?"

"The loop?"

I nodded.

He smiled his lopsided smile.

We were only supposed to walk the loop—around the small road, past the cafeteria, through a parking lot, then on a path between the big lawn and the large road, past detox, and on to the small road again—if we had three people to walk. Staff said it was for safety reasons, in case a patient went down with a heart attack or something. Then one person could stay with the victim while the other person went for help.

But we all believed it was because staff figured it would be tougher to go over the fence—to the nearest bar or crack house— with three rather than two.

Brendan had a loping, soldier's walk, despite having been shot in the thigh.

One time, when the guys in the unit were walking back from the gym, crossing the large road, Brendan had stationed himself in the center of the road, ten feet down, hands clasped behind his back, feet parted, shoulders back, stopping traffic. Even in a white tee-shirt, he looked the full Marine.

"So, pal," he said.

And I told him. The office, the pills, telling Kevin and Sam, the letter.

"Ah, prof. Paulie. You busted yourself."

"Indeed."

"God. God."

He was smiling in a complicated way. Sad and thoughtful and knowing.

"Now what's left?" he said.

We went past the cafeteria, and on to the blacktop of a big parking lot. We could see hills and farms and roads a long long way in the distance.

It was a steep downhill, and then we came to the path at the bottom of the big lawn.

"Right. What's left."

"'Cause isn't there always something after?" Brendan said.

"Ha."

Way up at the top of the lawn, between the end of the long low building and the stone building with the cupola, there was a terrace, and six or seven women were sitting and lying around in the sun. Juliet was there, and two lovely blond women named Amy and Ruthie, and three or four others.

They started waving and hollering to us—to Brendan, I imagined, and we waved back.

Brendan was smiling wide, and he said, "She likes me, Paulie. Swear to God, Amy likes me."

"Jeez, Brendan, what're you talking about?"

When we rounded a curve and passed out of sight behind some trees, he dug in the pocket of his jeans and fumbled out a much-handled scrap of notebook paper.

"Look. She gave it to Ruthie to give to me. Outside Chit Chit."

It was written in pencil, in a rounded, girlish hand.

"Dear Brendan,

"I have noticed you and I like you and I hope we can meet in the city. I am sorry to hear you were hurt in the war. That is very sad."

She listed her phone number, email, and signed, "Warm regards."

"Brendan, my God."

"She's beautiful."

"Brendan."

"I couldn't believe it."

His face was red and he was grinning.

"Please don't tell anyone."

"Course not."

I put my arm around him, squeezed his shoulder. And we walked. The day was warm, the sky high and cloudless. Pilots might have said that visibility was a hundred miles.

"You know, dude," he said, "I've been thinking."

"You gonna marry Amy?"

"Well that, yeah. Goes without saying."

"Knew it."

We were approaching detox, the other end of the long building.

"You know what happens with the pills, right? I mean, you've done that how many thousand times."

"Okay."

"And that always sucks."

I nodded.

"And you don't know what it is to do without them."

I nodded again, but Brendan was staring at the sky. Where maybe he could see a hundred, maybe even a thousand, miles.

17

The phone was black. The phone sat on the corner of Stan's desk. He punched some numbers, I pulled my chair in, and out of a speaker in the phone's base we heard it ring.

I pictured the phones in our house, the white one next to the piano in the entry room on the first floor, the black one on the bookshelves next to our bed, the phone on the bureau in Liz's office, under the Miro print. I pictured the rooms and the things in the rooms. Boy sneakers, a worn leather couch, curled and sleeping cats, light falling through gauzy curtains.

Something clicked, Liz said hello in a clear, bright voice.

We said, Hello, Hello, Hello.

How's everybody.

Everybody was okay.

"So extra time," Liz said.

I only had five days to go. The shaking and sleeplessness were pretty much the same as they'd been. I was thinking I was in for a long withdrawal. You just didn't do as many benzos as I'd done and get off them in weeks. I was expecting this to go on for months.

If I left Caron on schedule, I'd go on Sunday. Today was Tuesday.

"Extra time" sat in the room.

I almost ached and longed my way through the telephone wires, home.

"By the way," Liz said, "I got your note about the pills. They were there and I got rid of them."

I tried to read her voice, but she was matter-of-fact.

"I'm doing okay here," I said. "I really don't see the point of staying extra days."

She and Stan both started in. I was in withdrawal. Yeah, I could be in withdrawal in six months, but some extra time here wouldn't hurt. And I'd been so snowed when I arrived that I'd kind of missed the first days.

"I don't see the point," I said.

Liz didn't see the point of coming home too soon.

Stan started talking and got on a roll.

I couldn't believe Liz was saying what she was saying. I felt abandoned and betrayed.

I thought about hitchhiking out of here, but had no idea how to get home. Plus it would be tough to get rides—someone as big and old as me. I wouldn't pick me up.

"How long?" I interrupted Stan.

"How long?" Liz asked.

"A week," Stan said.

Liz said, "That sounds good."

"Three days," I said.

"Six days," Liz said.

Stan said, "Six days it is."

"Fuck," I said.

"C'mon, honey. We'll be down on the 20th."

I looked at Stan, at his watery eyes behind big black-rimmed glasses. I looked at his Buddhist prayer flags.

"You'll really come down?" I said.

"I'll really come down."

"You'll bring the boys?"

Stan laughed.

"Absolutely," she said.

Outside the window the trees were a deep June green. One of the staff golf carts went by, with Ronnie from Extended Care driving.

God, I thought. I was starting to know the names of staff from other units. And I was starting to remember names. I'd been here a long time. If weeks were years, I'd been here more than three years.

I'd had moments when I doubted I'd ever get out.

Other people, new people, were coming in all the time. And people I'd been here with for the whole run were leaving.

One of the new guys was D.B., who was just an inch or two over five feet tall, and who wore velour sweat suits. He had big feet for a little guy, big ears, and short hair. He had a handsome, angular face.

D.B. was a coke addict, a gambler, and he talked in rushes of words that were hard to understand at first, they came so fast and tumbled and spilled and washed over each other.

At every lecture and talk and meeting, when all of us were dying to get out of the room at the end to go smoke, walk around, talk, the speaker would check the clock and ask if there were any questions. The speaker would then look around the audience, and all of us, just about every one of us, would see D.B. twitching.

Ten seconds would go by.

Twenty seconds.

Thirty.

People were putting on their sweaters, folding their glasses.

D.B.'s hand shot up.

The speaker sighed because the speaker understood. The speaker wanted to go have a smoke too.

"Yes?"

"When you said that addiction was a disease, did you mean, I mean, did you mean, like was that something like a disease like cancer or diabetes, or more like kidney disease or a heart attack or a stroke or something? I mean, there's all kinds of diseases, and I was wondering what kind. Like one that can kill you? That kind?"

The speaker said, "It can kill you."

There was quiet.

D.B. twitched.

His hand went up.

Some people groaned.

The speaker nodded at him.

"When I came in here, that day, when I came in, I was kind of messed up, you know. Like pretty messed up. I guess a lot of people are. Everyone I guess. Right?"

The speaker shrugged.

"So what I was wondering," D.B. began, and people groaned more. People groaned loud.

D.B. plunged on.

"Does he know what the fuck he's doing?" Marcel whispered. "We're hostages."

I shook my head.

That same day, a sweet middle-aged guy came in. He was tall, had white hair and a beard, came from Virginia, and—swear to God—he looked like Robert E. Lee.

Richard became an instant legend because he had driven from home, and in the trunk of his car he had a green fifty-gallon trash bag filled with pain pills. OxyContin, Percocet, Vicodin, codeine. There were so many pills that it had taken two detox nurses several hours to count them before handing them over to the Drug Enforcement Agency.

Richard had serious arthritis, and in the following days, as he withdrew from narcotics, he was in constant pain and he slept less and less.

In small group, Matthias was our arbiter, our lawyer, our voice of reason. He wore bright orange V-neck sweaters, and said we could all visit him at his house in the Hamptons.

Toby starting saying that he was realizing more and more that drinking wasn't the only dangerous thing he liked to do.

Toby wore reading glasses that sat halfway down his nose, a black vest, and he usually carried a dark blue binder that he used to take notes. He had a barroom voice, and when Stan asked him what he meant, aside from drinking a bottle of whiskey and crashing his pickup truck into a utility pole, and walking away unscratched, Toby said in his sandpaper voice, "Well, Stan, you know, the usual stuff."

"What's usual for you, Toby, may not be usual for me."

Toby started talking about climbing eighty-foot trees in heavy thunderstorms, and diving off high cliffs into rocky reservoirs, and driving on highways at three in the morning, a hundred and ten miles and hour while dead drunk. Blind drunk.

"And lived to tell the tale," Matthias said.

Toby said he was so so alive when he did that stuff. Never more alive.

I said that that's what guys in combat talked about. The nearness to death brought a nearness to life.

"But keep doing it," Bowtie said, "you die."

Davy trilled. Huh huh huh. "We all fucking die," he said.

"So go out in a blaze of glory?" Stan asked.

"Or ignominy," Matthias said.

In a soft drawl, Richard said, "Live fast, die young, leave a beautiful corpse."

"Except the corpse would be pretty damn unbeautiful. Coming down from the tree, rocks in the reservoir, spin out on the highway at one-ten. Meat, baby," Bowtie said.

We all looked around at each other—Arnold, Marcel, Edmund, Matthias, Richard, Davy, the others. People glanced at each other, then looked away, and when I saw Doc next to me he had a somber face, and it occurred to me that he had worked on cadavers in medical school and he had worked for a while in a Medical Examiner's office. He'd seen the corpses. Up close.

D.B. said it wasn't ten to one you'd die. It was five to one, two to one, one to two. Then one to ten real soon.

Guys laughed, and D.B. smiled. He was pleased he'd said something everyone liked. Because at the end of lectures, when his hand shot up, guys had begun to pelt him with wadded up lecture notes. D.B. would duck his head, but it wouldn't interrupt his questions.

Then he said it was like Second Life.

Second Life was so fucking cool. And nobody got that. Nobody understood.

"Huh?" Doc said.

"Second Life," Sam said.

Marcel said, "Get with the program."

"The fuck?" I said.

"You guys live in a cave. God," Edmund said.

Judd, who rarely came to group, startled awake, and wanted to know what everyone was talking about. Tawking!

Stan asked D.B. to explain, and D.B. said, "A game. Computers. You get this new life. Like Sims."

"Sims?" I asked.

"What's Sims?" Matthias wanted to know.

"You fucking guys're hopeless," Marcel said.

"We have regular lives," Doc said.

"Real lives," I said.

"Well, sort of," Doc said.

So in Second Life, this game you played on the computer, you took on this whole, new identity. A wife and kids, if you want, a career, Stan said. A house or two, cars, a girlfriend.

"Or two," Davy said.

Ha ha ha, some guys said.

"They cost you," Stan said.

"How do you know so much about this?" Matthias asked.

"D.B.'s taught me all I know," Stan said.

"So you get this all-new life," D.B. said. "And it's way cool. So sweet. Like everything you every dreamed. And it's all right there, right there on your computer. And it's not just a fantasy, like some kid's game. Not like some X-Box shooting game. Cause I've tried them. Believe me.

"You have a beautiful wife and girlfriend, a family, a job. You have money, cars, a second house on a lake."

"What about your real wife?" Matthias asked. "You have one?"

D.B. was shifting in his seat. His hands and arms were moving.

"Sure," D.B. said. "Of course. Goes without saying."

"No it doesn't," Bowtie said.

"Kids?" Doc asked.

"Yeah, yeah," D.B. said. "Sure. Three."

"A house?"

Check.

"Job?"

"Sure."

"Girlfriend."

D.B. blushed, twitched. He looked down at his dancing hands.

"D.B.," Matthias said. "Girlfriend?"

"No," D.B. said. "In my dreams."

"In Second Life," Arthur said.

"House on a lake?"

He shook his head.

"Cars?"

"Two. But better ones in Second Life. And more."

"That's kind of messed up," Richard said.

"No, no, no no no, you don't get it," D.B. said. He started talking faster and faster.

Cause that's what his wife said too, and she didn't get it, and his boss, and like the whole fucking world, and they didn't get it. He meant, he meant, he could see the coke, that really fucked him up. All that money and the dealers, and the health shit, the legal shit, he meant, okay, that was really really—and he meant this—that was fucked up. Okay.

And that's why he was here. He admitted he was powerless. No two ways about it.

Plus the gambling. He meant, yeah, the fucking money, and the buzz, just like the coke. Jesus. He knew. He admitted.

"But Second Life, c'mon."

His boss warned him to not visit his girlfriend at work, okay, warned him a few times, then when he wasn't working, he had more time online.

Then his wife, the kids. He meant, for God's sake. He wasn't doing much coke, just staying online. Not sleeping too much, and when his wife was calling from her parents' house, the kids were fine there, they liked the pool over there, and sharing a room.

The pizza boxes were piling up next to the computer, the phone got shut off, but he was real careful to pay the electrical bill, and who needed to shave or any of that. Who could see him from the computer, right?

Doc said, "Dude, sounds like a drug to me."

"I gotta say," Edmund began, then he stopped.

Because D.B. was crying, and shaking his head slowly, and he was saying, "She was beautiful, so beautiful, so beautiful, and she understood. She really really got it. She did."

We were all quiet a while, and then somebody cleared his throat, and someone else coughed, and a few people shifted in their chairs. Crossed and recrossed their legs, folded their arms.

"D.B.," Bowtie said in a low soft voice.

"Hey, pal," Stan said.

D.B. went from shaking his head to nodding slowly, but the tears kept leaking from his eyes. They moved down his face and fell on the front of his velour track jacket, turning spots of blue darker. The spots grew bigger on each side of the zipper, and still, no one had much of anything to say.

Finally Bowtie began to talk, in a voice so low it was almost a whisper.

Bowtie said, "It's really tough, and it's really raw."

He said, "I've been doing this—my Lord—ten, fifteen years now. In other rehabs, in clinics, in prison.

"No matter where you go, and who you work with, the disease is pretty much the same.

"Blue haired ladies in Beamers, trust-fund dudes at Caron, lifers in a correctional facility, prostitutes, professors, anybody, it's pretty much the same thing.

"In prison," he said, "in maximum-security prison, you had some very tough guys. Some guys from the streets, from bad homes or no homes, or homes so scary the streets or gangs or foster care looked pretty inviting.

From shit, he said, that made his skin crawl. That he had never imagined, and he had imagined some pretty bad stuff, let him tell you.

And these guys had done bad stuff, and most of them didn't admit to very much. If they admitted to anything, they only did what they did because they had to. The other guy made them do it. They were provoked. Devil made them do it.

And a really big percentage of them were on drugs. Booze. They were fucked up when they did their crime. Or crimes.

No matter how bad the places they came from, the brutality they'd experienced, they would not have done what they did if they were not under the influence. Period.

But the other thing, and this is why he brought it up in the first place, is that once these tough guys were in prison, the biggest thing they feared, and the prison officials knew it, and it was the major disciplinary tool—was what?

"Anybody know?"

No one said anything.

Finally I said, "The hole."

"Thank you, Professor. I knew you'd come through."

"What?" Davy asked.

"Say it again, Paul," Bowtie said.

"The hole. Solitary."

"Solitary confinement," Bowtie said.

People said, Ah and Oh and Hmmm.

"First you go to Keylock, confinement to your cell, then you get the hole," I said.

"There you go," Bowtie said. "And everyone dreads the hole. You get in a fight, get caught with a weapon, with drugs, you disobey a C.O. enough times, break enough rules, you get thirty days, sixty days, in the hole, in solitary."

Edmund said, "No room service?"

No T.V.?

Computer?

Visitors?

Books? people asked.

Bowtie moved his head from side to side.

"Paul," he said, "what are the C.O.'s like in maximum-security prison?"

I laughed.

"Not real warm and friendly."

"What else?"

"They tend to not like or trust inmates, and vice versa."

"What's a C.O.?" Arthur asked.

"Corrections Officer," I said.

Marcel said, "Inmates call them cops or screws."

D.B. had stopped crying and was watching and listening.

"Why do you think solitary is so scary to all these tough guys?" Bowtie asked. "Like it's the one thing that can really get these guys' attention. You can't hit anybody, you can't have a shiv, you can't have drugs or booze, you gotta do what the C.O.'s tell you to do—you gotta obey the rules, at least most of the time—and most of the time it works. Cause you don't want to go to the hole.

"Guess what, gentlemen?

"You don't want to be alone.

"It's painful to be alone.

"It's brutal, it's unnatural, it'll make you crazy, it'll finally kill you.

"I'm not talking about some solitude. Reading a book, listening to some music, praying and meditating. That's healthy and good. You never get some alone time and you go crazy.

"But think of the hole. Think of solitary."

He looked around, from one of us to the next. We each seemed to be trying not to look guilty.

"Small steel cell. No windows or bars even. Steel door, steel slot so they can slide your food and water in, thin pad to sleep on, hole to crap and pee in. That's about it. Take you to a doggy run for a half hour a day of exercise according to state law, but you don't see anyone there, and you're in shackles.

"Then back to the hole.

"All day and night. Day and night, day and night, day and night. You and the steel walls and yourself.

"Think of it. You and yourself. You and yourself.

"Just thinking and thinking and thinking.

"All the time.

"Go to sleep to it, wake up to it. And really fast, you'd kill for human contact.

"Stay with that. With being that alone.

"Because we're social creatures. Like it or not, we need each other.

"Big, tough, ripped killer guys start crying and pleading to get out after a few days in the hole. Honest.

"The English novelist E.M. Forster said, Only connect.

"Only connect.

"That's huge. Connect to your work, your community, but especially to other people. If you can just do that, just connect, then you have a good chance with this disease, you have a good chance in life. And if you don't, the chance are not so good.

"And bear with me here, cause this might sound squishy, but underneath all this, the hole, connecting, is the matter of getting and giving love.

"Because booze and drugs cut you off. It's a big disconnect. Addiction puts you in the hole. It makes you profoundly alone.

"You lose your job, wife and kids leave, pizza boxes pile up, stop shaving, but you pay that fucking electrical bill cause that's what powers the computer, that's what feeds the addiction.

"And she was beautiful, she understood. That pill, that drink, that shot, that snort, that bet, that purchase—it delivered. It gave you that sweet, warm feeling. And that feeling—let's face it—that feeling in the first hour, the first time or times, maybe the first year or two even—of addiction, feels like love.

"I have no doubt in my mind that everybody in this room loved their substance of abuse truly and deeply. Loved it with all your heart and all your soul. Gave it everything.

"Gave it tons of money.

"Gave it marriages.

"Houses.

"Cars and trucks.

"You gave it broken bones, your livers, your septums, your brains.

"Guys, you gave it your children.

"Your honor, dignity.

"Your minds and spirits.

"Your integrity.

"But the thing with love," he said, "is that it has to be reciprocal.

"And ask yourself, and go slow here, be really careful.

"What did it do for you?"

He sat back and looked down, and all of us looked down.

We sat in utter stillness, almost listening to the blood move toward our weaving hearts.

18

There was a pile of mail on the dining room table, and the cats mewed and rubbed against our legs as we came in. The curtains were drawn, the air was stale, and everything looked familiar and strange. And we'd only been gone a week.

The kids were itchy, were tired after a long day in airports and on planes. We'd only flown from Knoxville to Ithaca, with a two-hour layover in Pittsburgh. Five hours, with another two hours in cars.

But that was on top of most of a week at Grandma's, where everything was different, there were no friends, and the kids had to be careful about—well, everything.

Tennessee was red clay earth, Baptist and Presbyterian churches, brunch at the country club Sunday morning, and good manners. Nobody swore. People were so nice that after a while you began to long for New York, where nobody gave a damn if it was so nice to meet you.

The mail was rolled newspapers, magazines, rejections from magazines for stories and poems, a bill or two or three, a few postcards, an invitation or two, junk mail, then a ten-by-thirteen brown cardboard envelope with stamps from overseas. From the Middle East or India or somewhere.

It was almost flat, with what seemed like thin packets of index cards inside.

What? I thought.

What the—?

Then I remembered a few weeks earlier. Was it that long ago?

On the third floor, not down here on the first floor.

Very late at night, not in the middle of the afternoon.

In darkness, not full daylight.

Not when Liz and Austin and Liam were right there, but when I was totally alone.

And it seemed—God, it seemed so improbable, so impossible, so crazy. That you could go to a web site, hit a few buttons, type in your name and address, give them your credit card number, and there, along with magazines and bills and post cards, you got— what?

I was shaking with excitement. Valium. Had I ordered Valium? Or Ativan or Klonopin? Xanax?

I said I had to check e-mail, took a few bills, one or two post-cards, went to the sanctuary of the third floor. My hands, my legs, everything, trembled.

And sat at my desk without even taking off my coat. Took the really sharp scissors with blue handles, carefully cut the very edge of the envelope, which was thin cardboard, and sat.

Grew strangely calm. Just paused for a surprisingly long time.

Was giddy for a moment or two. Thinking that if this was real, that if this was, say, one hundred 2 m.g. tablets of Ativan, that would be so much more than a single prescription of .25 m.g. That was eight hundred .25 pills.

The very number staggered me.

But it couldn't be true, couldn't be real.

Maybe they sent me newspaper, or sugar pills, or packets of index cards.

But if they meant to rip me off why send anything at all?

I finally reached in, felt—newspaper?

But—

There was something in the newspaper. There was definitely something in the newspaper.

I slid it out, and there was newspaper in some foreign language—Arabic? Urdu? Sanskrit?—carefully folded. I unfolded it, and inside was black carbon paper. Inside that were taped aluminum and plastic blister strips of pills.

Blue Valium.

Each strip had ten pills, and on the inside aluminum part was printed, in two languages, the Roche logo, and Valium 10 m.g.

My heart lifted and swelled.

It had the damn Roche label, for God's sake, I thought.

But watches on the streets of New York City had the damn Rolex label.

How stupid was I?

Well, very stupid. I knew that. I said as much that moment. You just put fake Rolex watches on your wrist. You put Valium you bought off the Internet in your body. Whether it was rat poison, sugar, the ground bones of yak.

Who knew?

But so much of me felt smart as hell. To do an end run around the doctors with their meager scripts. To do an end run around the whole world and every person and thing in it for not giving me what I wanted when I wanted it. Here I was, self-contained, with all I needed.

I cut three pills from the strip, took one, swallowed it without water.

I checked my watch. Three-twenty-two. I should be feeling something by quarter of four. Maybe I'd be sick by then.

Maybe I'd be delivered to some soft, warm place.

With the other two pills in my pocket, I went downstairs, sorted through mail, brought our luggage to the second floor, was putting away clothes, bags, feeding kids, reading to them, when a warmth began to spread through me, that melting feeling, and it wasn't from the closeness to my two beautiful red-headed sons.

The Valium from that country somewhere in the world was the real product.

I was fucking high.

"Hey," Brendan said, and Edmund said, "What's happening?"

I looked up from my chair at the Butt Hut as though coming out of sleep.

Eddie said, "Short timer. How short, dude?"

"Three, four days," I said.

Eddie was wearing a white button-down shirt, something you didn't see around here.

"Why you dressed up?" I asked.

Edmund looked at Brendan, then at me. He pulled at his gray sweatpants, pointed at his untied sneakers.

"Dressed up?"

Brendan started laughing.

"Dressed up?" Edmund said again.

"The shirt. The power shirt," I said.

He said. "C'mon. You've seen a shirt like this. Haven't you? Where you live?"

"The swamp," Brendan said. "Dude lives in the swamp."

Dude?

This felt like detox suddenly.

"How long you been here?" Edmund asked.

"Too long."

"Tell me," he said.

"A life or two."

"We'll miss you, Boss," Brendan said.

A few days or a million years ago I'd been banging into walls, calling everybody John or Matt or Tom. Now I'd been here longer than anybody on Men's Primary, and it did and didn't feel like it.

The shakes, the weird raw feeling, the not sleeping, were as strong as ever, but I'd been over a week, ten days, maybe twelve days, without a single benzo, and that was shocking, that was not a thing I ever expected to do.

Stan showed me a photo of myself taken in Admissions the day I came in, and I cringed and laughed.

I was wearing a blue ski jacket, even though I never skied, my hair was very long and dark and surrounded my head like a hood, and my face was a mask. It had a gray-blue color, the fixed expression to the mouth and jaw.

But the scariest thing was the eyes, which were far away and doll-like.

It was worse than a mug shot because there was no sullen anger, no rage, no shame or anguish. Everything about me in the Admissions photo was numb, departed.

When I saw myself in a mirror now or reflected in a glass door, I was all nerve and raw air. I was walking on my toes, my hair was short, my lips twitched and trembled, and my eyes were clear, scared and dark with life.

I asked Stan to get me a copy of the photo, and he said he would, on one condition.

I looked at him.

"Don't show it to your family, especially the kids. You'll scare the shit out of them."

So Bert was gone, Tim, Ricky and Max were gone. Alan, Raphael, Toby, Arnold, Doc, Jake and Chuck were gone. So many others were gone too, Matts and Toms and Erics, guys whose names I couldn't remember, or guys I hadn't been very close to.

I liked the new guys, or most of them, and was tight with Edmund and Brendan and Matthias. I usually ate with Davy, of all people, because he was always sitting by himself in the cafeteria, and I didn't mind his trills and tics.

Davy might seem strange at first, but he was sharp and funny. He wasn't like anyone else in here.

I had begun to realize that one of the big things about Caron, one of the principal forms of treatment, aside from lectures, meetings and group, was that they took you out of your addictive environment, took away everything, and they gave you—each other.

And you hung out with them, talked with them, ate with them, smoked cigarettes with them, argued with them, sat through meetings and groups with them, got along with them.

You got to see their strengths and weaknesses. They drove you crazy, but you got to like them. You heard so much of what they had gone through. How much they had struggled.

As you had.

And you began to see that you had a great deal in common with them.

So much like Alcoholics Anonymous. A fellowship.

Because addiction was about loneliness.

Isolation.

So much of Caron was about intense bonding with fellow addicts.

And that was like decades earlier, when I came out of a state hospital, pure nerve. I was twenty-three years old.

I went to AA almost daily for about three months. I read the Big Book several times.

The meetings were held in church basements and recreation rooms, in community centers and hospital meeting halls. Around Boston in those days, the program was overtly religious, had an Irish-Catholic flavor, and was less receptive to drug addicts. There was a slogan they hung on the wall, Keep it simple, stupid.

Not the compassion a beaten-down addict was seeking.

I also saw an alcoholism counselor at the Mt. Auburn Hospital in Cambridge, and began to take Antabuse, a prescription medication that prevents the liver from metabolizing alcohol. You take one Antabuse pill a day, and you cannot drink for twenty-four hours. If you take even a half teaspoon of alcohol on Antabuse you get violently ill. Severe headaches, vomiting, abdominal cramps, diarrhea.

I stopped going to AA and took Antabuse for five straight years, then off and on for another five years. I had no side effects, and it helped start me on twenty-five years clean and sober.

During that time I went to college, worked three years with deaf-blind teenagers, went to grad school, got married, taught college, had two sons, wrote books and articles, taught in prison. I had friends.

But perhaps the one thing I was missing in my life, the most important thing I was missing, was a fellowship. My friends were nearly all writers, professors, therapists, artists and lawyers. None of them were in recovery.

And the funny thing is that even during my three months in AA in Boston, despite the religious tinge, I liked the rumpled people in the program. They were often generous, tolerant, interesting and funny.

They were people like the guys in Caron. And if I couldn't find much to like in them, I couldn't find much to like in myself.

The thing I heard over and over and over at Caron was: Don't drink or use. Go to meetings.

Don't drink or use. Go to meetings.

Don't drink or use. Go to meetings.

I once asked Bowtie, walking up from lunch, "What do I do when I leave here?"

"You tell me," he said.

"Don't drink or use."

Then together we said, "Go to meetings."

"Do those basic things," he said, "and I guarantee, everything else will follow."

So Stan and I went over my Aftercare Plan.

AA meetings. Appointments with a psychotherapist. Appointment with doctor. Appointments with the Alcoholism Council and the Department of Mental Health.

Exercise and good nutrition.

The other crucial thing was that Liz and I would switch offices. Instead of me being on the third floor in isolation, I would take her office on the second floor, off our bedroom.

It was a converted sleeping porch with a cathedral ceiling, big windows that looked out onto the trees in the backyard, and in a place where there was far more traffic than the third floor. Liz and the boys would be in and out of the office all the time, the desk was fifteen feet from where we slept, and there was no steep flight of stairs.

The other crucial thing was that Liz put drug filters on all the computers in the house, programs that made it impossible to access drug web sites. They were the same kind of programs that parents used to block porn sites from kids.

None of this was guaranteed, but it put speed bumps in my way. It was a little like not keeping alcohol in the house or not going to a bar. Or avoiding, as the Catholics said, an occasion for sin.

Then it was two nights and a wake-up.

Everywhere I went on Men's Primary, everywhere at Caron—the gym, cafeteria, Chit Chat, lounge, meat locker, my bedroom or bathroom—I kept thinking, Well, this is it.

No more sitting in Chit Chat forever.

Only five more meals in the cafeteria.

No more visits to the gym.

Two more sleepless nights in that bed.

Two meditations in the meat locker, one more small group.

Everyone I had known and come in with was gone. And when Sam, my roommate, left four or five days earlier, it was especially tough because he had come in a day or two after me, and we'd been together the whole time.

Like me, Sam had a basically solid marriage, good kids, a good career, enough money.

Whoever had decided to make Sam and me roommates had thought carefully, because we both said that our asylum from the asylum was our small room.

When I saw Levon coming to and from the cafeteria, he yelled and waved, and usually stopped to talk. But he was with a group of guys from Extended Care—Larry and Peter, Blake, George, Rodney—and he looked somehow different, better shaved, shirt tucked in, almost a civilian.

They got to go on field trips, Levon said, and outside meetings, so he'd been sailing, and God, get this, he'd been to a bookstore.

Word leaked back that Bert lasted no time at all.

Someone from Caron took Bert to the airport in Philadelphia. The driver parked, helped him with his bags, and as soon as Bert was able to "shake the motherfucker," in his words, he hit the airport bar.

He did make his flight back home, and he did tell people from Caron that he was drinking, but his post-Caron sobriety was measured in seconds and minutes.

Nobody had heard from Chuck or Tim, but Raphael was in a group home near Baltimore and doing well, and Arnold and Doc were hitting meetings together in and around New Jersey and New York City.

During the last few days, I kept thinking of my mom and dad. The staff had asked me about drinking in my family when I was growing up, but there was none.

My father was a teetotaler, my mother might have had a beer once or twice a year, if that. They worked, they took care of their kids, they were devout Catholics. They were small, shy people.

My mother was born in Bellevue in New York City, was orphaned at age eight, and grew up in a Catholic orphanage in Tarrytown, across the road from Pocantico Hills, the estate of John D. Rockefeller.

My father grew up in a blue-collar family in Newton.

They met on a Catholic Worker farm in Ohio. The Catholic Workers were Christians who were devoted to the principles of economic and social justice.

When I was nine or ten years old, my great-uncle, Paul Emmanuel, for whom I had been named, died, and there was something a little odd, a little off, about his death.

He was my grandmother's brother, and he lived alone in a house in Watertown, one suburban city over from us. His wife had died ten years earlier, and he was retired from a desk job at an insurance company.

The few times I'd met him he didn't seem especially friendly. He was just a heavyset older guy with iron gray hair, big hands and less to say than me. His clothes were wrinkled, and there were yellow stains down the front of his white shirt.

He also smoked unfiltered cigarettes, Luckies, and he had a deep and frequent cough.

A couple of years before his death, Uncle Paul lost one of his legs.

When I first heard this whispered between my mom and dad, I thought he had misplaced it. Under his bed, in a closet or the basement or garage.

But then I learned his leg had been amputated, above the knee, because of infection. He hadn't taken care of a smaller infection in his foot; it had spread; and to keep the infection from spreading to his entire body and killing him, his leg had to go.

I imagined him in his white stained shirt, a Lucky with a long ash dangling from his lips, watching people work on his infected leg.

Then he died of a heart attack, alone in his house in Watertown. There was a funeral, but my brothers and sisters and I didn't attend, and nobody, not my father or mother, not my grandfather, not even my grandmother, who was Uncle Paul's sister, seemed especially upset.

A few weeks later, with my father and uncle and grandmother, I went to Uncle Paul's bungalow in Watertown to help clean and pack.

It was a brown stucco house on a leafy street, and it was September. There were cars parked here and there, but no people in yards or sidewalks.

The whole project, going to a dead guy's house, going to the house where he had died, spooked me.

My grandmother unlocked the front door from a ring of keys that had tags on it, and the heavy front door squeaked.

The light inside fell through pale curtains, and everything was brown and tan like old photographs.

There was a hallway with a coat stand, stairs going up, and to the left a living room with a dark sagging couch, two lounge chairs, a coffee table, bookcases, and everywhere, crowded ashtrays, and stacks and stacks of yellowing newspapers and magazines. There were flat empty bottles tucked between books and newspapers, between the cushions on the couch, even a few under the edge of a rug.

Off the living room were the kitchen, which was piled with crusted dishes and empty cans and bottles, a small rounded chugging refrigerator

Everything smelled funny. Musty and closed up, but something different too. Something like garbage, but like vinegar and maybe medicine.

I went up the creaking stairs, which curved to the left. There was a hallway at the top, and a string hung from a light in the middle of the ceiling. A cracked plastic bird was tied to the end of the string.

There were three small bedrooms and a bathroom, and only two bedrooms had anything in them. In one was a single bed, covered by an afghan with a pattern of black and white diamonds. There was a sewing machine, a desk and chair, and bookcases packed with books.

Then I noticed, wedged between and behind many of the books, clear and amber bottles of varying sizes and shapes.

Many of the bottles were empty, but some had liquid in them. Clear liquid, tan liquid, dark liquid.

Sometimes just a quarter inch. Sometimes two or three inches.

I took a bottle from between two books—How To Win Friends and Influence People; Riding the West—unscrewed the cap and smelled it. I pulled my face back fast.

It was powerful. It smelled like something that, if you lit a match to it, would explode.

The other room had a big bed, two dressers, a few chairs. I went in, walked to the far side of the bed.

There was a lamp on one tall dresser, a brush and comb, a box for jewelry.

Then in a corner of the dresser, I noticed a photograph in a silver frame. I picked it up, but it was so dusty that all I could make out were two figures, a man and a woman.

I wiped it off with my tee-shirt, and there was a couple, probably in their thirties, standing in front of a bungalow. They were dressed up, maybe for church or a wedding, and they were smiling big toothy smiles. The woman held the man's arm.

Then it hit me like cold air. The bungalow was the house I was standing in. The smiling man was someone I had known. He was someone I was named for. Someone I might have been like.

19

It took my father a long time to die. It took forever. It went on and on and on—so much longer than any of us, my brothers and sisters, my mom, the doctors, thought it could go. On my last full day at Caron, I thought of him. Lying alone that morning in my too-small bed, for hours I thought only of him. He'd been dead twenty years.

My mother had told me that she'd sometimes come upon him in their otherwise empty house, and he'd be sobbing—on a sunny May morning, on a gorgeous afternoon in August—and when she asked him what was wrong, why was he crying, he said he didn't know. He was just—he didn't know. He may well have known, but she never did.

He always took perfect care of himself, was lean as wire, but he had a disease called central and obstructive sleep apnea, which meant that his brain did not tell his body how to breathe effectively, especially when he slept. In his sixties the condition worsened; whenever he got a cold it turned into something much worse, usually bronchitis. When he was 68, it turned into pneumonia, and he was soon on a pulmonary intensive care unit in a Boston hospital, fighting for breath.

I was in Ithaca teaching, finishing the semester at Cornell. My classroom looked out onto the Arts Quad from Goldwin Smith Hall, and the trees and bushes, the forsythia, lilac, oaks, maples, dogwoods and magnolias, were turning the quad Edenic.

Already, I was beginning to miss the students, who were talking about summers in Italy, Colorado, New Jersey, the Bay Area, Maine, Singapore. They would hike, sightsee, teach tennis, wash dishes, waitress, work in a state legislator's office.

They were writing papers about a mother's breast cancer, their terror of open spaces, about a brother's suicide, about locking themselves in the bathroom, sticking their fingers down their throat and throwing up again and again, until they weighed less than ninety pounds. They wrote about getting drunk, getting naked, and going into dark bedrooms with people they hardly knew. Then doing the same thing the next night and the next night because that felt like love.

They often wrote about things they had never told anyone in their lives, and I was moved, I was shaken, I was honored.

My older sister called from Boston and said, "He's not gonna make it. He doesn't have much time."

So I arrived in Boston, late in the second week of May. Twenty years, to the day, before I'd arrive at Caron.

He was in a private room on the sixth floor, a ventilator attached to the tracheotomy in his throat, making the suck-click-hiss sound of a machine breathing.

He was spectrally thin. His skin was paper, his bones sticks, and the sticks pressed the paper. His ears and hands seemed enormous, were tinged blue, and his arms were tattooed with bruises from being stuck with needles.

His wrists were tied to the railings of the bed because in delirium he pulled lines and tubes out.

The staff had brought a cot into the room for the family to rest, because this was serious waiting now. This was waiting for the end. One or two of us were there all the time, at ten in the morning, seven in the evening, but especially at one or three or five in the morning.

My father had always been quiet and unassuming and virtually friendless. He was four or five inches over five feet, maybe a hundred forty pounds, and he had big kids who were successful and loud and had loads of friends.

And it went on, day by day by night by day by night. It didn't stop.

And we—mother and wife and children, sisters and brothers, sons, daughters— we were there, spending more time together than at any period since childhood. Holding our dad's hand, talking to his expressionless face, pushing the hair off his forehead.

We walked the sixth floor halls, hung out briefly in the waiting area near the elevators, and sat leaning against each other on the cot in his room.

We went home only for a short time, to shower and nap.

At four in the morning, in his room alone, tired and standing at the window looking out at city lights, I watched a delivery truck pass below, then a cop car, and then the glowing street was empty. The silence on the street, in the room, had a positive charge.

This was his last gift to us.

His death.

He was pulling us close to him and to each other, and showing us what it was to die. In this quiet, slow, dignified way. As he lived.

It wasn't easy and it wasn't pretty. It involved pain and doubt and anguish.

His death brought us deeply into one of the central mysteries of life. And it had a dark beauty.

Years later, when my first son was born, there was the same kind of exhaustion, pain, fluids, and a cutting to the center of life.

For my father, the end came finally just before six on a gorgeous Sunday morning in June. One of those clear mornings when the air seemed to shine.

My brother and sister were with him when his heart stopped. Then they called my mother and me.

We drove to the hospital, and my mother did not seem sad, just very tired. She pointed out various flowers and bushes that we passed, and said, Beautiful.

On the sixth floor, my brother and sister had already taken the lines and tubes from my father's body, and shut off the vent. The room seemed utterly quiet without the suck and click and hiss.

I almost didn't notice or recognize him.

His body was taking on the characteristics of death, the waxy skin, the gray tint.

We bent to kiss him, and then we stood and were silent a while.

Standing there, I thought of Liz. I thought of her sleeping, back in Ithaca, in our apartment, with a cat curled at her feet.

We had been talking for some time about having kids. We had been talking about it the whole time we'd been together. First I wanted to and she didn't. Then lately, she wanted to and I had begun to think, Not so fast.

Standing there in that sixth floor room, early on a Sunday morning, it felt like everything was different, was new, was a collection of things I no longer understood.

In the meat locker that final Friday night, for my last meditation, Matthias read something about miracles of change in people's lives. He read in his careful and clear Manhattan attorney's voice, enunciating each syllable and comma and period. Then a new guy, Jonny, J-O-N-N-Y, read the prayer of St. Francis.

Jonny was a tall, lean guy with the skin on one side of an arm and half his face scraped off. He'd fallen from a bicycle at three in the morning, on Martha's Vineyard, while—go figure—smashed on booze and benzos.

Jonny missed about a third of the words.

"Where there is ha...ha..."

"Hatred," Davy said.

"Thank you," Jonny said.

"Where there is hatred, let them soon lo...lo..."

"Let them sow love," Judd said.

"Thank you," Jonny said.

"Let them sow love," Jonny said.

"Never thought I'd be teaching a fucking Catholic prayer," Judd said.

I'd been sitting there every night for thirty-seven nights, not counting my time in detox, and it was my favorite thing in the Caron schedule. Ten or twelve guys sitting in a circle in this windowless, featureless room. End of day. Day is done, gone the sun. A few readings, guys talking quietly in turn, a final reading. A little music and nature sounds, an ingathering for the Serenity Prayer.

Richard said he was an addict. He said it had been a good day. He said he'd miss the professor, who was a real decent guy, but he was sure the prof would do great.

Just about everyone else said the same kind of thing. Then Davy laughed and trilled. The lunatic Davy laugh. He said he didn't know what the fuck people were talking about. The prof was a real dick, the prof was dumb as a post.

We laughed and laughed and I said, "Thanks, Davy."

Brendan said, "Any words?"

I shook my head.

"Just thanks," I said. "I'll remember you."

The music came up on the boom box. Harps and flutes, a synthesizer, then birds and flowing water. The room went completely dark, so dark you couldn't see anything. The sounds swirled and flowed, moved up and down and around, and Edmund, who was operating the box, kept it on for a while.

My chin was on my chest, and I felt more relaxed than I had in a while. The tics and tremors were gone somewhere for the moment. I was nodding, was following threads of sound, the trickle of water over rocks, the cheep and twitter of birds, a string plucked, and I was adrift somewhere, was almost floating, and this wasn't Valium or Klonopin, this was natural, God help me.

Then the sounds started to fade, the light came gradually up.

Guys were blinking, guys were yawning.

Jonny had fallen asleep.

Brendan said, "Bring it in," something I'd first heard from Alan, the tree climber, five weeks earlier.

Where was Alan? How was he doing?

We stood in a tight circle in the middle of the room, eleven or twelve of us.

Brendan said, "Paul, you wanna take us out?"

We had our arms around each other. Tall guys, short guys, medium guys.

"Left foot back for all the shit we leave on the mountain," I said.

Everyone moved their left foot back.

"Right foot forward for all the good things to come."

Right feet went forward.

"Heads held high, they've been down too long."

Guys lifted their heads.

"Who's the Higher Power who sees Amy in the shower?"

"God," everyone said. "Grant me the serenity, to accept the things I cannot change, the courage to change the things I can, and the wisdom to knooooowwww the difference."

Outside it was misting, and there were a few people huddled in the gazebo. I went over to the edge of the gorge to stand under trees and smoke, and there was a new guy there, a guy I'd never seen. He had long black hair and rimless glasses.

As he smoked his hands trembled. He seemed to have trouble holding the cigarette to his lips.

"You okay?" I asked.

He nodded.

Then I said, "I know that's a damn stupid question. You're shaking pretty bad."

He smiled grimly.

Then he looked at me. "You're shaking too," he said.

I looked at my hands and they were moving like I was in a car at high speed.

"You know what's fucked-up?" I said. "I'm leaving tomorrow, after thirty-seven days."

He nodded, took another trembly puff, flipped the butt into the wet trees. Then he stood and shook and shivered.

"I just came up from detox."

"I figured."

"How could you tell?"

"You remind me of me."

"Ah."

"Benzos, right?"

He nodded. He didn't even look at me. He didn't ask. He knew I knew.

We stood in the mist, not saying anything. Stared into the dark woods. Water dripping and slapping, washing the world.

Stan had talked to Liz in the morning and she was indeed coming.

"She's definitely coming?" I asked.

He nodded and smiled. He kept smiling.

"Stan," I said. "Jesus."

He looked at me and smiled.

"Why you smiling?"

He laughed his booming laugh.

"You thought she wouldn't come?"

I'd thought a lot of things. I'd thought of them telling me I'd have to stay an additional three months. Or that I'd be taking a bus to Ithaca, and that I'd be meeting Liz at her lawyer's office. Or that they had a rented room with a hot plate all ready for me, above a pool hall somewhere, with a neon sign that blinked, VACANCY, VACANCY, VACANCY, all night long.

"Fuck, Stan," I said. "I don't know."

"She's leaving around five today," he said.

"Today? She's driving today?"

Stan nodded.

"You serious?"

He kept nodding.

I wished he'd say something, and wondered if this was some kind of test.

Stan's office was four doors down from the meat locker, and had about as much character. Aside from his prayer flags and a small Buddha, his bookcase contained mostly what looked like manuals about manuals.

"So she'll be here?"

"Tonight. Around nine or ten."

"With boys?"

"I believe so. And they'll be here for you around nine in the morning."

I had cleared out the drawers in my room, and packed everything but my toothbrush, and there wasn't much to do except imagine Liz and Liam and Austin in the car, driving through rain, coming down here to get me. I pictured them at some nearby hotel in Reading, or Wernersville, or wherever we were in the rainy mountains of Pennsylvania.

In some room with two big beds, a television, a remote. There was no television at home, so the boys loved to flip through channels and watch whenever they could.

Liam would control the remote, and would go mostly for sports, for football, baseball, basketball, lacrosse, swimming, luge, hang gliding—anything that moved.

Then Liam would get up for the bathroom, to open the door and look down the hall, to check if there was anything happening outside the window in the parking lot. And Austin would grab the remote, Austin would start clicking.

He'd go for music and music and music. He'd go for science fiction stuff; if there was a droid or spaceship, he'd pause. He'd check out war movies or history shows, and he'd pause at sports, but just briefly.

Then Liam would try to grab the remote, but Austin was quick.

A year earlier that would have worked. Liam could have easily overpowered his little brother. He'd been doing it all his life, not that he was a bully or even unkind. It was just the drill. Pure animal protocol.

Now Austin had grown, much of it in a year. He was pushing six feet, and though he was wiry, he lifted weights, and was surprisingly strong. He was the second best arm wrestler in his grade at school. He even beat Kanya, this girl who was huge, and she was scary.

"I'm not even kidding," he said.

And Austin suddenly started playing lacrosse, and he was good. He loved it. So when Liam would try to muscle the remote from Austin, Austin would curl up around the remote and Liam had to use his words.

Which is exactly what they told him to do in daycare: Use your words.

And Liz would be curled up in a corner of one bed, reading a book, or checking e-mail, and Liam, finally, would say, "Mom, he won't give me the remote."

"Shut the thing off," she'd say, which is what they knew and feared she'd say.

So they did, and then would bum money from her to get stuff from the vending machines in the hotel lobby.

They were doing that. The two tall red-headed boys. Walking down a hall, talking and joking, having promised their mother they wouldn't get soda cause it had caffeine, and thinking that in the morning—

What were they thinking?

The mist turned to drizzle during the night, and it was the longest and shortest night. I thought that it would have been great to be able to talk with Doc, but if I lit a smoke he would have given me twenty reasons why smoking was an assault on the human body. It would have been a kick to have a few cigs with Levon or Chuck, but they were gone.

Everybody was gone.

Pretty soon, I'd be gone.

Then light was coming in the window next to the bed, and it was, five, six, it was time for breakfast.

The C.A. Dave said, "Good luck. If you need anything, lemme know."

The rain picked up.

I had my bag, plus a green trash bag of dirty laundry. I left it near the outside door next to the clock tower.

The rain slowed to a drizzle, stayed that way a while, then picked up again.

The whole place it seemed was in a lecture or meetings, and I walked around, and it was odd, but the place, the program, had already moved on.

Matt the C.A. took me down to Admissions in a golf cart. The windshield wipers were going but didn't work much, so water streamed down the glass.

Then down below, next to detox, we stopped, got out, took bags from the cart. I thanked him.

I got my bags through a set of double glass doors, dropped them, and in a peculiar way, almost didn't notice or recognize them.

How tall, what red hair, what fair and glowing skin, and eyes that were alert, alive, shining, eyes that had so much in them.

I thought of more than three decades earlier, when my father came to pick me up at Medfield State Hospital. Most of my family had not visited me. More than anyone, my short, quiet father did visit. And there he was in the end, standing in the front dayroom of ward R-2, asking how I felt, me nodding, both of us smiling nervously and awkwardly, saying little.

Because what was there to say? Neither of us knew what would happen. All we had was hope, and a small prayer.

Now, thirty-two years later, my dad was dead.

And I was a husband, I was a father.

The three of them, Austin, Liam, Liz, stepped forward, and surrounded me. We put our arms around each other, the four of us, grabbed each other, held on.

For the moment and the day. For the duration, it seemed. For life.

About the Author

Paul Cody was born and raised outside Boston, has degrees from the University of Massachusetts - Boston and Cornell University, and is the author of four novels, including *The Stolen Child* and *So Far Gone*. He has taught at Cornell, Hobart & William Smith Colleges, and the Colgate Writers' Conference, and in Auburn Prison. He lives in Ithaca, New York, with his wife and two sons.

Acknowledgements

I'm deeply grateful to John Lauricella, Lauren Smythe, Ted Everett, Ed Hardy, Julie Schumacher, Stuart O'Nan, Martha Collins, Lamar Herrin, Liisa Grigorov, Eric Webber, Mary Cody-Kenney, Pete Wetherbee, Missy Bank, and everyone at Caron, especially the boys, my brothers, on D-Block. And I'm especially and always grateful for Liz and Liam and Austin, who move the sun and the moon and the stars. With thanks and hope and love.

Made in the USA
Lexington, KY
21 July 2013